# DAVID
# FFRANGCON-DAVIES

*His Life and Book*

Yours faithfully
David Ffrangcon-Davies

# David
# Ffrangcon-Davies:

## HIS LIFE AND BOOK

*by*

MARJORIE FFRANGCON-DAVIES

*with an introduction by*

ERNEST NEWMAN

LONDON
JOHN LANE THE BODLEY HEAD

*First published in 1938*

PRINTED IN GREAT BRITAIN BY
UNWIN BROTHERS LIMITED, LONDON AND WOKING

*To*

CONSTANCE MacCOLL

*and*

DUGALD MacCOLL

*great gratitude*

*for invaluable help in the
preparation of this book*

# CREDO

*Have we lost Paradise, our high content*
*And ageless ecstasy?*
*What though the busy ages teem,*
*Dreaming old dreams in sombre night,*
*And aeons through strange races pass*
*In coloured pageantry from star to star,*
*And suns dissolve in symphonies*
*Making new worlds as men ascend!*
*Only I know that birth and death are dreams,*
*And through the heart's November and the lonely graves*
*Some instants hold you and your voice.*

MARJORIE FFRANGCON-DAVIES

# INTRODUCTION

## by Ernest Newman

THERE WAS A good deal of misunderstanding of Ffrangcon-Davies's *The Singing of the Future* when it appeared in 1905; and in that misunderstanding, if my memory does not betray me, I had my small share. Later readings of it, combined with a wider experience of concert and opera singing, have convinced me that from the beginning Ffrangcon-Davies had hold of the right end of the stick. It would have been surprising, indeed, had it not been so, for he had within him everything that was necessary for the task he had set himself in his book: he was a fine singer, who had worked unceasingly at the conquering of technical vocal difficulties, and he was too thoughtful and sincere an artist to imagine that the be-all and end-all of singing was to win an audience's applause by beauty of voice alone; he regarded himself in the first and last place as the servant of the poet and the composer he was interpreting.

The point with regard to which misunderstanding was most frequent in 1905 was his apparent inversion of the order of importance of the three main factors in the singer's equipment: he was supposed to be opening the door to the rankest amateurism by maintaining that if you think correctly and speak correctly you need not worry about such a trifle as the technical mastery of tone. The careful reader of his book will soon discover that Ffrangcon-Davies—as might have been expected, indeed,

ix

of a singer who was himself possessed of so beautiful a voice—never had the least intention of disparaging good "singing" in the ordinary acceptation of that term. What he was driving at was that excessive concentration on what is called bel canto—blessed word!—either in study or in performance, results, and must necessarily result, in the formation of a mere half-singer at best. I am not going to take sides here on the thorny question of 'voice production,' of which, as the reader probably knows, there are to-day to least a hundred 'methods,' each of them not merely the best but the one and only. I would be the last to talk slightingly of the results of the immense amount of skilled study, especially on the physiological side, which has been given to that subject during the last generation or two. But I enrol myself under Ffrangcon-Davies's banner when he goes into the fight with his cry that bel canto in and by itself is not enough.

Nay, my experience as a concert- and opera-goer has convinced me not only that it is not enough, but that in the absence of something else—and what that something else is it is the main purpose of this book to show us— concentration on bel canto can be more of a curse than a blessing. The pure and simple bel canto vocalist (I have some scruples about calling him or her a singer in the full sense of the term) is manifestly incapable of doing more than a fraction of the job demanded of him. Having concentrated solely on 'tone production' from the beginning of his studies, he can produce, by the time he comes before the public, a more or less beautiful tone. But it is often beautiful more in the abstract than in the concrete: it has the minimum relation to the task set before him by a particular composer, or in particular portions of a given work. I speak feelingly on this subject, for hardly a week goes by without my having occasion, in the course of my melancholy duties as a music critic, to lament the sheer incompetence of four singers out of five in everything that lies outside this holy ground of 'tone production.' Having learned to 'place' their tone in a particular way, with a view to obtaining purity, roundness, power, flexibility and all the rest of it—highly desirable things in themselves, I need hardly say—they find themselves unable to 'produce' their tone at all except by means of a certain shaping of the mouth and a certain direction of pressure. The results of this limitation are many, and all of them are dire. Every note they sing at the same pitch is precisely the same in colour, regardless of the fact that the same note ought to have a different tinge in different phrases according to the sentiment of the words that accompany it. One gets tired of telling these good people, in one's notices of their performances, that while they produce tones that fall quite pleasantly on the ear they not only reduce every song to the same common denominator of intellectual and emotional milieu— Strauss's bright *Ständchen*, for instance, being rendered with precisely the same tones and tone-colours as Brahms's veiled and mournful *Immer leiser wird mein Schlummer*—but they make every song sound as if it had been written by the same composer.

Further, they have the most obvious difficulty with their diction: vowels in general are distorted in order to allow them to 'place' the tone according to precept and habit; certain vowels, at certain pitches, become the merest caricatures of themselves; consonants, especially final consonants, are neglected because they involve an adjustment of the tongue or lips which interferes with the adjustment of the mouth in general required for the kind of tone they want to produce. Some of our most admired coloratura sopranos are woeful offenders in this last respect: even in Italian, the language of the most frequent and the 'purest' vowels, their handling of the words is often the merest fake. In languages like English or German the diction of the average singer is deplorable. As Richard Strauss has pointed out in the preface to his opera *Intermezzo*, getting one's words across is mainly a matter of the consonants: a properly formed consonant, he says, speaking as a conductor with a vast experience, will cut through the most brutal orchestra, whereas the most powerful singing tone even on the most propitious vowel —'ah'—is easily drowned by the mezzoforte of the ordinary opera orchestra of 80–100 players. (This, incidentally, is the main reason why Mime is the one character in the *Ring* whose words are always intelligible; as the singer of the part is not usually a belcantist, he is free to concentrate on the crack and bite of his consonants).

Now Ffrangcon-Davies, being an exceptionally intelligent singer, realized a fact which, rudimentary as it is, appears to have escaped the notice of most vocalists, for whom singing is a matter of 'voice production' and little more—the fact that as composers do not write mere vocalises in their songs and operas and oratorios, but set their music to words and try to make the expression of the music match the expression of the words, it is the prime business of the singer to identify himself with this dual expression so that the full force of it will come home to the listener. If that is not done, what earthly sense is there in the composer trying to establish the utmost intimacy of connection between words and music, situation and music? Hence Ffrangcon-Davies's insistence that no one is really worthy of the name of singer unless, in addition to producing melodious sounds, he can also, in the first place, make the words perfectly clear to the listener, and, in the second place, let his imagination play upon both words and music in such a way and to such an extent that *not only his words but his tones* are one in accent and in colour with the specialized emotion of the song he is singing or the operatic part he is playing. Even in such a language as that of Italian opera, which is a constant invitation to the singer to achieve bel canto and just leave it at that, a great artist like Caruso took care that tenor parts of completely different characters were sung by him in completely different styles. He himself has told us that when he had to sing a simple part, such as that of Nemorino in Donizetti's *L'Elisir d'Amore*, he would spend the morning and afternoon of the day of performance sinking himself in the pyschology of the part, so that there would be no danger at night of his turning upon the music the tremendous resonance and the brilliant colours that he would use for a heroic rôle such as Radames or Otello.

The supreme exemplar, however, of the type of all-round singing that Ffrangcon-Davies had in mind, and which he prophetically foretold, was Chaliapine, who had mastered every element that goes to make up the complete singer to such an extent that not only could he differentiate as no other opera singer has ever been able to do between one part and another, but he could produce a pure singing tone with his mouth in any position. He could abandon himself so completely as he did to the meaning of the words, the meaning of the music, and the colour of the situation because he had mastered singing in the way that Ffrangcon-Davies has sketched, in this book, as the ideal: he could give us the purest bel canto when required, delighting us by the roundness and richness of his 'cello tone and the grace of his phrasing, but he could also, when required, shape his mouth for the expression of irony, of hatred, of disgust, of a snarl, and still *sing*. He began as Ffrangcon-Davies says the student should begin, by 'singing thoughts'; his incomparable singing art had been developed 'under the guidance of linguistic and imaginative thought'; he made the listener hear 'what author and composer felt when placing their creations on record.'

So I commend, without the slightest desire to disparage the study of bel canto within its proper sphere, this book of Ffrangcon-Davies to the careful attention of young singers who want to make their art complete. But let them not imagine, as many people did in 1905, that Ffrangcon-Davies's desire was merely to make the path easier for the earnest amateur. They must not get it into their heads that in order to sing well all they have to do is to speak well; as he himself says, 'singing and speaking are *not* synonymous.' But they can rest assured that until they speak as well as they can sing—and no singing can be technically too good—they cannot hope to have their lyric or dramatic imagination perfectly free to play upon what they are singing, and so become ideal 'interpreters' of the composer and the poet.

I would like to add to this Introduction a word of appreciation of Miss Ffrangcon-Davies's biography of her father. It is of the profoundest psychological interest to those of us who, while Ffrangcon-Davies was alive and active among us, could see him only from the outside, in his public capacity: we now have some idea of the spiritual travail he had to undergo as an artist, and precisely because he *was* an artist. I have been struck also by the tact with which his daughter has treated certain aspects of his later life that had to be set forth frankly for complete veracity's sake. The letters from and to Elgar I have found particularly interesting: we see now how much the Elgar oratorios counted for in Ffrangcon-Davies's development as thinker and artist, and how much these two fine spirits owed to each other.

ERNEST NEWMAN

# FOREWORD

THAT THE TIME has come for the publication of a revised and abridged edition of my Father's book, *The Singing of the Future*, I am convinced by the repeated inquiries received, not only in this country, but from America and many countries in Europe where David Ffrangcon-Davies is remembered and beloved.

So many books, systems, and suggestions relating to voice-production—which he himself would have condemned as dangerous and misleading—have followed on the publication of my Father's natural and straightforward teaching (a teaching that can be used either entirely on its own merits, or else alongside any other sane method of voice-production) that a return to the instruction and idealism he so fully justified in his career as a singer seems indicated.

Many years spent in studying his book and following his ideals, conscious, as he was, of the inevitability of the artist's mission, and also with a vivid memory of the unparalleled beauty of his voice—have convinced me that my Father succeeded in discovering and writing down the processes by which a singer may achieve his goal, illustrating all the faculties necessary for a perfect art-performance.

That he succeeded not only in his song and in his book but in his life also, and in spite of all that he suffered, I have long believed; and in writing a short sketch of his character and experience my aim has been to join to the memory of the artist, whose work both practical and prophetic is assured, the memory of the man beloved by many.

In his preface to *The Singing of the Future* the late Sir Edward Elgar wrote of my Father's book that he hopes it may date 'a commencement of that long-desired new edifice of English music which will some day be raised by those—and by those only—who have seen the most of truth.' That this great man, himself a visionary and crusader in the world of art, has placed his friend in such a category, sets a standard to which I willingly conform in seeking to give a just account of my beloved Father in his conscious pursuit of a life-purpose and ideal which he summarized thus: 'To think closely and to bring our thoughts to a focus, so that we are absolutely unconscious of all surroundings; to know and see mentally nothing but what we have decided to concentrate upon, that is the essence of all fine effort, in life and in Art.'

MARJORIE FFRANGCON-DAVIES

*21 Kensington Court*
*London, W.8*

# CONTENTS

xix

# CONTENTS

# ILLUSTRATIONS

# PART ONE

*David Ffrangcon-Davies:*
*His Life*

*by*

MARJORIE FFRANGCON-DAVIES

# I

DAVID THOMAS DAVIES was born at Bethesda, in Caernarvonshire, on December 11th, 1855, and the rich influences of his race, tradition and environment stamped him from first to last a Celt. Blue mountains fold on fold where the sheep browse through the summer uttering their lonely cries; passes where the echoes roll and, in the winter, the mists soar; waters that foam to still lakes; paths that climb to the white farmstead and the small grey church, whose leper window shows where the poor doomed came in olden days tolling their warning bell; there the far horizon of the sea and foaming shore with waves that come and go—advance, recede, eternally; valleys and winding streams; woods centuries old prisoned in ivy, and miles of waving moorland—Loved Land of light and shade, of storm and calm, of beauty and magic—all this is Wales, and this was his heritage.

The family was originally named Edwards and came from Denbighshire, tracing descent through a line of well-connected farming landowners to the early sixteenth century. My great-grandfather, Dafydd Edwards, moved with his brother Evan to Llanfairfechan in Caernarvon, where they began, after the Celtic custom, to name their families patronymically by the Christian name of their father, Dafydd.

My grandfather, Dafydd Dafis, was born on a farm at Clynog Fawr, but left home as a young man to make his way in the Penrhyn quarries and foundry at Bethesda—a splendid figure of a man, tall and of fine carriage, proud in the birthright of his race. Working at the foundry all week (he was known there and is remembered as 'David Davies, the Foundry'), Sunday saw him in frock-coat and top-hat with Gwen, his wife, in chapel.

Gwen Pierce, my grandmother, was of gentler disposition, with none of her husband's rigid severity; a contented nature and home-loving; lovely to look at, lovely to live with, so my father found her. Joseph, her firstborn, having died at the age of nine months, and her second child being a daughter, their son David came as a great joy into their lives; in him Dafydd and Gwen centred their dearest hopes.

To educate his son the father augmented his income as overseer at the mill by giving piano-lessons, which, although he himself could scarcely play at all, appear to have been remarkably successful. But it was Gwen, the sensitive and intuitive mother, who steered the current of that young life; she had the time to love and teach, and few changes came to disturb the peaceful home in which she lived for the greater part of her married life.

Mount Pleasant was one of two stone houses built for the overseers at Penrhyn Foundry. To the right of the front door was a small parlour, where many a youngster besides David learnt the rudiments of music. To the left a large roomy dining-room held an air of welcome and comfort. Out of this room opened a small scullery; then the kitchen where Gwen's rocking-chair faced the window. There, as she rocked and dreamed, it was borne in upon her that David had a mission. Recognizing the quality of pure emotion which surged in her son, mysterious, recurrent, wild yet controlled as the tides of the sea, she knew that it must one day bear upon its crest some treasure to lay at the feet of men. In his instant response to the beauty and mystery of Nature, she found the promise of a greater quickening. It was she who marked his first intuitions, set his first standards and upheld his vision and who taught him to love the Bible and to believe in it.

Yet Gwen had also a practical nature. Though there was never money to waste, no child came to Mount Pleasant without receiving a 'piece' of home-made cake or a mince pie; home from school you found her free of the fret of housework. Though her gowns were few, her taste did not err; here a ribbon, there a bunch of flowers on her bonnet, reminded her menfolk that she was their lovely one. They throve under her love.

David's first school cost a whole twopence a week, which included the use of the old harmonium, on which he practised assiduously; nor could the teasing of his chums alter his ways. He was a bright boy and a hard worker, so that he passed his examinations well and was promoted from the village school, a stone's throw from his home, to Friars School, at Bangor, where he learned Latin and Greek. He did not, however, outgrow his home. Dressed now as a Friars scholar, he still carried his mother's can to the shop for barm (it was bought liquid in those days, for the making of bread). 'David,' said the village, 'don't you mind carrying that home, now you are so big?' 'Mind! Why should I; anything for my mother.'

And everywhere he sang; in chapel, in church choirs, among his friends, alone in the hills. There are people still who remember the exceptional quality of that young voice. Rarer still was the quality of his imagination. It was to his mother he confided his boyish absorption in the prophet

Elijah; Elijah walked by his side as he roamed the hills, peopling them in fancy with strange hosts; Elijah who first fired him with the desire to shake the sluggard world from its lethargy. It was this strong wise mother who, seeing the development of her son taking him far beyond the local horizon, urged him to go into the Church. Though he early leaned towards a musical career, her son's art lost nothing by the years that he gave to the Church, but gained immeasurably in depth.

So David went to Oxford. Many sacrifices were made for the high hopes his parents entertained of his future. Before he left his home David added to his own the name of his favourite haunt in Wales, the Nant Ffrancon Pass near Bethesda, and was thereafter known to his family and friends as Ffrangcon. Life was kind to him at Oxford. The utterly genuine character he had developed under the loving guidance of his parents made him a great favourite; he possessed a boundless affection and saw no reason why he should hide it. His friends called him 'The pocket Adonis,' for he never grew to be tall like his father, but took after his mother both in looks and figure. He was something of an athlete, too, and rowed in his college eight, entering whole-heartedly into everything he did. He came home to Bethesda having fulfilled the ambition of his parents with the degree of B.A. in 1881, from which he later graduated as M.A. and was now ready for the career that had been urged upon him.

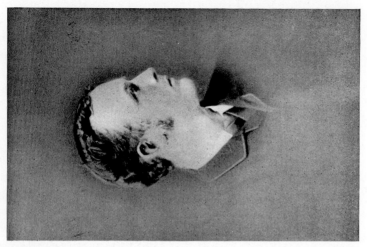

Taid, Nain and David (aged about 10)

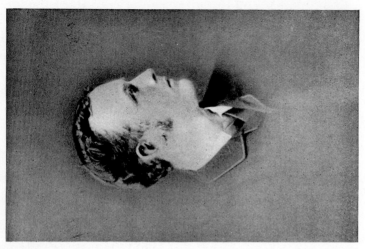

At Oxford: the Pocket Adonis

# II

FFRANGCON WAS ORDAINED deacon in the Church of
England in Llandysilio Church, February 18th, 1883, being
ordained priest by Bishop James Colquhoun Campbell of
Bangor a year later, and so began his ministry in Wales.
Here was ample scope for his energy, intelligence and
devotion, for a while at least. A good deal was expected
of a clergyman in those days, and Ffrangcon was a hard
worker. He was appointed to Trevor, near Pwllheli, in
Caernarvon, where to this day parishioners recall his
ministry with gratitude. Here stands the whitewashed
farmhouse where he lodged, and on whose lawn every fine
summer evening he collected his choir, conducted, taught,
sang, and at the same time played the rackety harmonium
which he carried about with him. Here, too, his friend,
Hugh Williams, came every evening for a chat after his
work at the quarry. Very proudly this old man told me,
'He used to compete for the singing prizes with me; *but
he always won!*'

His was the unconscious singing of a man whose heart
is in his song; the spontaneous work of a man with a song
in his heart. There were no empty pews when Ffrangcon
preached or sang. True, he emptied the chapels—but in
return he sang for them, as he also frequently did at St.
Anne's Church, Bethesda, where he had formerly been a
choirboy and his parents now attended. Was there a
family in need, he emptied his pockets and scarcely knew

5

he did it—so spontaneous was his giving. 'We were lost when he went away,' the old people have told me, 'a fine-looking man, with his curly black hair and fair complexion.' But Ffrangcon took his vocation seriously, and, not content to remain a village curate, he did all he could to equip himself for a higher step.

It was whilst he was curate at Conway that he first met my mother, Annie (Nan) Frances Rayner. Her father, a Manchester doctor, had built himself a house in Conway valley. He died, unfortunately, soon after Bryn Rhedyn was completed, but his daughters spent much time there and the young curate came often to visit them, or to wander in the evenings over the Conway mountains, or, more often still, to sing. 'Nan' must have been a very lovely girl, and there is no doubt that in all the years to come beauty, romance, Conway and my mother were inextricably woven into a single pattern in his mind. She lost her heart to him also at this time, and was so bold as to buy a photograph of the young minister displayed in a shop at Llandudno.

During these years Ffrangcon had been studying the organ under Dr. Rogers in Bangor Cathedral and often deputized for him when he went away. Hearing that a vacancy had occurred for a minor canonry in the cathedral, he was urged to apply for it, and after an interview was assured that the post was as good as his. To his bitter disappointment, however, the vacancy went to another. This was a turning-point in his life. There and then he determined to enter upon a musical career and to fulfil his dream of becoming a singer.

He knew, however, that if ever this goal were to be achieved, years of technical study and hard work lay before him; he also fully realized that whilst it was easy enough to hold to a vision of loveliness in the familiar atmosphere of Wales, a call to life amid sterner surroundings was essential to the cultivation of his faith and purpose. He therefore applied for a curacy in London and was appointed to one of the poorest districts—St. Mary's, Hoxton. His duties here were made easier for him by the warm sympathy and support of his vicar and by the many friends he made. He threw himself unreservedly into the work of an East End curate, learning of life in its more sordid and degraded aspects. Of this time he writes: 'I got some of my finest tones here, and learned some of the things which made my "Elijah." '

In his spare hours he studied voice-production with Mr. William Shakespeare, who seems to have been a wholly admirable teacher and an invaluable friend. So Ffrangcon followed his star, encouraged by the unswerving loyalty of his beloved parents, who in old age relinquished their deeply rooted fear that disaster would follow if he left the church for the stage. Visits to Wales were few, for the work was unceasing and much was at stake from 1887 to 1890. Letters from Bethesda, bringing him reminders of the home to whose influence he owed so much, were solace to him during the busy years of his apprenticeship.

'Taid,' my grandfather, was still at work, his hair whiter, his temper shorter, but pride in his son a satisfying thing, for his horizon was unconsciously broadened through his son's forward steps. Supervising the loading of a ship at Port Dinorwic one day, he heard some people speaking London English, almost a foreign language to the old Welshman. Eagerly he questioned them: 'You come from London?' 'Yes,' was the answer. 'Do you know my son, Ffrangcon-Davies?' 'No, but London is a large place.'

Proudly the old man said: 'That may be; but there is only one Ffrangcon-Davies.'

In the autumn of 1889 'Nain,' my grandmother, began to fail: she would not allow them to tell Ffrangcon lest he should grieve, so that when the news of her illness and the shock of her death came, it found him unprepared. She was buried on the fourteenth of January 1890 in the little churchyard at Llandegai. Her son Ffrangcon was a broken man.

How much he had built upon her love, how greatly he had leaned upon her gentle strength, he had not known until he lost her; and now a grief so desolating numbed him that he cried with his prophet friend, 'Lord, now take away my life!' To a crowded church he had preached his last sermon in London—as he had preached his first in Wales—on the subject of Elijah. He stood at last on the threshold of his new career, and now at the moment of fulfilment the very mainspring of his energy and desire was broken within him. Many years later he translated from the Welsh, and set to music, the hymn,

> *Waiting through the long night ever*
> *For the dawning of the day,*
> *Waiting till the portals open*
> *And the chains all fall away.*
> *Come and lighten thou our darkness,*
> *Come, thou morn of Jubilee. . . .*

And across it he wrote: 'A favourite hymn of that proud, strong, gentle soul whose power I knew not while she was yet on earth.'

# III

FFRANGCON'S FRIENDSHIP WITH Nan Rayner, begun in those happy days at Conway, had continued throughout the London period; news was exchanged from time to time, though Ffrangcon's letters gave little hint of the changes which were taking place in his life, or of his own reactions to those changes. His mother had his entire confidence. With her he was himself, and there was nothing strange in his imagination, hopes and dreams; she neither marvelled at nor was made self-conscious by them. In the eyes of both his parents his simple mission was to prove that God's word is with power. Taid once wrote, in a letter to his son: 'I believe in music, that it has the greatest power for civilization; *if properly conducted and worked out to that direction, it is the right hand of Christ's religion.*'

It was after his mother's death that his friends in London, helpless to comfort him in his grief, wrote and urged Nan Rayner to exert what influence she could. He sang in Manchester a few weeks after his loss, and Nan—more beautiful than ever he had remembered her in the three years of their separation—seemed to him when they met after the concert to be an angel straight from heaven. Little though she could fathom the depths and causes of his agony and loneliness, her heart went out to him; and that night they became engaged.

Three months later they were married in the old Gyffyn parish church. Part of the honeymoon was spent at Cardiff, in the home of Madame Clara Novello Davies. It was natural that Ffrangcon should have brought his bride to this, his second home, for the association established there three years before was to last all his life. It was in 1887 that he had first met Madame Clara staying at St. Davids, Pembroke. Anxious to turn to good account the opportune visit of two such talented artists, the town persuaded them to give a concert, the proceeds of which were to be devoted to the lighting scheme—with, I believe, such complete success that St. Davids became, and was ever after, a veritable blaze of light!

Madame Novello Davies was prominent in the musical life of Cardiff, and she hastened to introduce her new friend to her husband, that stern critic, John Davies, in the hope that he might agree in her estimate of what she considered a beautiful discovery. Ffrangcon was invited to stay at Cardiff for this purpose, and chose as his test piece 'It is enough,' from the *Elijah*. From this time forward a friendship was established which survived every separation of later years. He was immediately invited to sing at a series of Saturday popular concerts, for which these friends were responsible; this was virtually the beginning of his professional career and here he received his first fee as an artist. In later years, when his friends' now famous son, Ivor, was added to this happy family circle, my father never ceased to take a keen practical interest in him.

It was before Ivor's time, however, and at Cardiff that Nan was received with open arms. Ffrangcon was deeply in love, and his wife responded to his need of her, caring for and watching over him with great devotion; but a shadow of misunderstanding dimmed their happiness from the first—which grew imperceptibly with the years. She had been brought up in a restricted environment and was

by nature unemotional. Ffrangcon had felt the Spirit that
bloweth where it listeth; his reserves were not with-
holdings, but unexhausted stores, and his emotions as
necessary to him as his ideals. Nan, too, found his serious
absorption in his work perplexing and his ambitions
dangerous; but to Ffrangcon his art was his goal—he must
attain it, whatever the cost.

How safely he might trust his intuitions was proved by
the result of his determined first appearance as the Herald
in *Lohengrin*, which occurred a few days after his marriage.
When the moment had come to make the decision regarding this really important step, he felt compelled to go
against the advice of his teacher, who predicted certain
failure if he attempted a dramatic part. My father describes
this struggle and its outcome in his book (see p. 95, *post*),
and adhered ever after to the conviction that the voice
becomes the servant of the mind disciplined by a high
idealism; for having put this theory early to the test he
never wavered again.

The phenomenal success with audience and Press alike,
in such a relatively small part, forced the conclusion that
his artistic instinct was deep and that he had grasped the
vital principles of his art. His teacher, Will Shakespeare,
wrote to him in recollection of their stormy parting: 'I
fear we were both excited; I was needing a holiday—you
had every reason to be so, as I am sure you had some
mental strain, what with the Carl Rosa offer, and the
difficulties of beginning rightly what I feel must be a
brilliant career.' Sir John Stainer also sent him this
message: 'I assure you I most sincerely wish you success
in the sphere of work into which you have so bravely
plunged.' In the months that followed, first appearances
in the *Messiah*, Brahms's *Requiem*, *Ivanhoe*, *Judas Maccabaeus*,

and other standard works saw the vindication of his ideals beyond all question, and audiences and Press alike were impressed by his sincerity and vivid and original approach to his work.

In October 1890 he sang for the first time the part of his beloved Elijah at the musical festival in Hovingham, Yorkshire, and if his rendering on this first occasion was noticeable, it later became unique. He went one day to Mr. Sims Reeves's studio for the purpose of taking the part through with that great artist. Pacing the room in his green carpet slippers, Reeves suddenly stopped short and asked him: 'What do you think of Elijah, Mr. Ffrangcon-Davies; what sort of a man was he?' My father laid his copy on the piano: 'If you'll excuse me, sir, I think he was a *damned old Radical*.' No flicker passed over the old singer's face; but he waved his pipe with a stately, 'Proceed, Mr. Ffrangcon-Davies,' as though the answer had met with his approval.

My father himself once wrote: 'It was for years the subject of my diligent study to enter into the spirit of Elijah. I wanted to *be* the Prophet who broke the rocks: to sing the music as it had never been sung before.' His must be a complete identification with character, mood and atmosphere in the minutest detail; he felt it to be a sacred duty laid upon him, as the interpreter, that he should recreate for the public the truth in the heart of poet and composer. Against the vulgar worship of the voice, and the idea that greatness lies in the capacity to sing a semitone higher or a tone lower, he always rebelled. His voice was to him an instrument quite profitless unless used for the clear expression of a thought or emotion. His Celtic temperament fired him to quick enthusiasm and a passionate dramatic sense, which his scholarly and reigious training held within the bounds of just expression. He was not afraid to stir the feelings of others by the frank and noble usage of his own, to stir ideas by ideas; he was nothing if not original; to him art was more than a senile following of outworn examples, and he courageously re- fused to be bound by merely traditional conventions. He knew that sincerity in singing could only come from con- viction faithfully followed, and an intense feeling demand- ing utterance.

Life therefore did not unfold easily for Ffrangcon, and the need of being always at concert pitch, added to his increasing responsibilities at home, made him nervous and highly strung. Those who are daring enough to insist on finding an expression that is true for themselves have a hard battle to wage. No pioneer on any quest walks lonelier than the artist or the saint. For his uncharted steeps there is no friendly camp fire till he has climbed the peak —and having climbed it, another beckons and he cannot rest till that is reached. Heaven is his goal; he may pursue, he cannot capture it; he needs eternity for its attainment.

Yet all along the way Ffrangcon was making his own charts and observations; there was no trickery or fraud about his pure technique; he could explain and teach it. In 1896 he went for the first time to America, and wrote to Nan, as he landed in New York: 'My first letter to you from the New World! And my first act in the New World is my letter to you; for did you not open out new worlds to me, when you decided to set sail with me?' His success there too was instantaneous, and from that date he re- turned each year, and sometimes twice a year, to fulfil engagements. He loved America, and America loved him and helped him considerably in the realization of his ideals.

In 1898 he wrote home: 'All is going as I wish and all the best men speak of my work as profound.'

Mr. Krehbiel wrote of him in the *New York Times*, after a performance of Mendelssohn's *Elijah*: 'Finely sustained, steadily and intelligently developed, the dramatic interest was superior to any I ever heard, thanks to the superb impersonation of Mr. Ffrangcon-Davies. The man sang with an earnestness that was positively inspiring.'

Ffrangcon formed happy associations in the States with Frank and Walter Damrosch, Emil Paur, director of the Boston Symphony Orchestra, Theodor Thomas, Anton Seidl, and many others. Each season saw a widening of the horizon and a growing intensity in his work. A desire to benefit by the artistic thoroughness of German musical culture drove him in 1898 for the first time to Germany. Writing to Nan from Berlin, after singing the Amfortas music through at a rehearsal: 'The conductor,' he says, 'a pupil of Wagner's, said it was wonderful; my knowledge of the power of Wagner's music, and my singing of it perfect. He said: "That is singing which cannot be done by the Germans; he sings better than the Germans"; the Orchestra applauded wildly; I didn't know if I was on my head or on my heels!'

So much work poured in that he sent for his wife and children to join him in Berlin, which became for several years their home and centre—though Ffrangcon continued to visit America and to tour all over Europe. He quickly and completely mastered the German language—an accomplishment more rare in those days than it is now—and his Lieder recitals took by storm that highly critical capital. The international reputation he achieved within ten years was certainly unique and a fine tribute to his work and vision.

Many were the friends who loved the man and reverenced his art. Herr Felix Weingartner has reminded me that amongst his own early compositions are songs he wrote for Ffrangcon-Davies; his memory and estimate of my father's work is most moving. Arthur Nikisch was also his friend; and Siegfried Ochs, conductor of the Berlin Philharmonic, considered him the greatest living Handel singer and also wrote of the Bach *Mass in B minor*: 'I never heard the extremely difficult part so splendidly sung in my life, and I am sure I shall never hear it better sung than by Mr. Ffrangcon-Davies. He was the first soloist ever able to make a German audience believe in the beauty of the "Quoniam tu solus."'

He had proved his method and technique beyond all doubting, and now his ideas were crystallizing into words. Ffrangcon had begun his book.

# IV

THE PUBLICATION OF Ffrangcon's book, *The Singing of the Future*, in 1905, by John Lane, The Bodley Head, was by far his most ambitious, though it by no means constitutes his only, appearance in print. Poems, articles, letters, reports of his lectures, were freely published before that date, each proving that it came naturally to this exact and thoughtful student to express well what he thought worth expressing. To a man accustomed from his childhood to the poetry of the Bible and the songs of his race words were a spontaneous medium for music and speech. Both in this country and in America Ffrangcon was frequently invited to speak and write on various subjects of interest (chiefly, but not exclusively, on music and on Wales), and the expression he gave to his opinions still makes very good reading. He wrote, in verse, admirable translations from many languages of the songs on his own programmes (though he always sang them in the original), and his original poems form an invaluable index to his character.

In that 'One Word More,' which Browning appended to his group of poems entitled *Men and Women*, he says:

> . . . *no artist lives and loves that longs not*
> *Once, and only once . . . to find his love a language*
> *Fit and fair and simple and sufficient—*
> *Using nature that's an art to others,*
> *Not, this one time, art that's turned his nature.*

*Ay, of all the artists living, loving,*
*None but would forgo his proper dowry,—*
*Does he paint? he fain would write a poem,—*
*Does he write? he fain would paint a picture. . . .*

Just so did Ffrangcon, and he turned from song to verse when he was greatly moved, not by love alone or 'only once,' but by so many things, that we come near to discovering him in his poems. First, beauty moved him: night in Wales, a storm at sea, stars, silence, colour and light and rain. Love moved him too, and sacrifice, devotion, charity and grace; earth touched him less than heaven. His pencilled verses, scribbled in trains, on programmes, on the backs of envelopes, show his need for self-expression, to 'find his love a language fit and fair and simple and sufficient.'

In none of his letters—except, perhaps, to Edward Elgar—does Ffrangcon speak openly of what ghastly forces ruin human lives. In conversation also he seldom dwelt upon man's inhumanity to man. Of the two poems he wrote to Madame Adelina Patti in 1896 after he had stayed at Craig-y-nos, one is about the beauty of her home, the other about the beauty of her nature expressed on the occasion of a charity concert in aid of the poor—at which he had himself assisted.

In America in 1901 he wrote a poem, of which the following is an extract, to one of the friends with whom he frequently stayed:

*You kneel in prayer, and every star is still*
*And every spirit stays its glorious flight*
*And turns to gaze upon you as you pray.*

. . . . . .

*Pray on, that futile wars may cease! Pray on*
*That men may wage a never-ending war,*
*Unhampered by self-pity, on themselves!*

.  .  .  .  .

*Not all the hate*
*Which hurts the heart, or sears the timid soul*
*With iron heated tenfold in the flame,*
*Can hold that Love away. . . .*

The death of an old friend moved him, not so much by a sense of his own loss as with a desire to keep his memory alive. 'We hear thy voice,' he writes,

*Through gathering gloom; and from the shore*
*Whereon, alas, stalk nothingness and night,*
*Thou sendest back, to cheer us to the end,*
*Thy spirit voice: 'Quit ye like men,*
*The victory's worth the strife! The pit is bridged*
*And all may walk with God.'*

Ffrangcon's most important poetic 'work' was a poem in blank verse, containing some three hundred and thirty lines and covering twenty-eight pages, published in 1907 by W. Speaight and Sons, Fetter Lane, and entitled *Per Aspera ad Astra*. Apart from the consistent sincerity and nobility of this poem, it has instants of picturesque and vivid beauty which illumine like flashes of sheet lightning the fine perspective of the author's thought.

To quote from the poem, taking from their context the more striking passages, is anything but satisfactory; yet the following may give some impression of the moods which he portrays—visions and dreams, unattainment and failure:

*How often, in the unremembered years,*
*Since men and worlds came from the womb of time*
*To labour and grow old, have tired eyes*
*From queenliest roses sadly turned away,—*
*Ears only thrilled, while sombre harmonies*
*Moaned on in music, heard when all is still,*
*O'er grass-grown failures and decay. Ah me,*
*'Twas surely in some other world than this,*
*I heard one say existence teems with joys,—*
*The busy thrusting of the silent seed,*
*The full warm colour of the ripened fruit,*
*And aspiration and the winds of God. . . .*

Apart from his poetic efforts, the most characteristic of Ffrangcon's writings are his courageous arguments with those critics with whose expressed opinions he felt conscientiously bound to disagree. His own definition of a critic—if it is original—is worth quoting: 'A critic is one who thinks he knows and *knows* he only thinks he knows.' In February 1898 the *Boston Herald* devoted two columns to an article he wrote in defence of the stage, after an attack made upon it by a very eminent critic in the English Press. With the same sincerity with which he took up the cudgels for his fellow-artists, he took them up for the art he served, and of which he would have considered himself a singularly unworthy devotee if he had not known that he knew (at least) as much about it as any critic.

That the personal aspect of criticism never engaged him is evident, but if he disagreed with the point or principle of criticism of a performance in which he had taken part, he expressed his opinion with force and eloquence, showing the earnest and philosophical view he took of the great works he was engaged in rendering.

When his book, *The Singing of the Future*, came out in August 1905, it gave a fuller expression to his already well-known theory and practice. He found the ground 'over-run with empiric theories' on the subject of voice-culture, and his first sweeping gesture was to clear the way for a greater simplicity and sincerity in art and a greater culture and profundity in artists.

His straightforward and natural method of teaching brought upon his head the anathemas of many teachers of singing and elocution, for it reduced their complicated systems to absurdity. His honest plea for greater versatility, even for universality, in the work of singers prodded a protest or two out of his more indolent fellow-artists, satisfied to win applause by means of one-sided repetitions. That, however, was only to be expected, for such practical idealism as his made its appeal then, as it does now, rather to the disciple in art than to the sycophant.

By serious artists and students the book was welcomed, and to them it remains a standard work. If it created a greater stir than its author had ever anticipated, it was because it bore the unmistakable stamp of authority. Here was a man who had proved through many years his ability not only to sing what he taught, but equally to teach what he sang; his opinion had weight and was heard with interest.

Letters from strangers as well as friends poured in from all parts of the world and many new contacts resulted, but to Ffrangcon himself the most valuable appreciation came from those who knew by long experience how sincerely he had practised what he preached. Amongst these was Rutland Boughton, who, introducing a series of three articles on the book in the *Musical Standard*, wrote as follows:

Let the reader quite understand how much my word is worth in this case. I have the pleasure of the author's friendship. In spite of that fact I write this review—nay, because of it, in a great measure. Only a man's friends, who know his everyday life, are in a position to judge how far his words are true words; only they are able to say whether he writes because he lives and knows, or because he would delude his readers by a fantastic falsehood of life and knowledge for the pittance of their praise and pocket. I *am* in a position to speak in this matter. I know the author writes of what he himself has experienced . . . that his art is bound up with the elemental forces of nature—which alone can justify a man in his singing, or writing, or reviewing, or anything else. Because the art of Ffrangcon-Davies rests on those elemental laws, and because he deliberately places it at the service of his ethical ideals, it is of importance to us musicians, whether we sing, fiddle or blow bagpipes.

When my father wrote to thank Rutland for these articles, he answered:

It is no credit to a man to speak the simple truth . . . but none the less it pleases me to think that I can do my mite of work in the cause of human progress. If one creature will get your book on the strength of my review it will have been worth the doing—not because the book is yours, but because *it only*, of English musical literature yet published, sings Resurrection!

Those reviewers of the book who had so much as a

word to say in criticism could be counted on the fingers of one hand, and to each adverse critic my father replied with great good humour. *Truth*, for instance, in an interesting and appreciative article, objected to the sometimes 'oracular character' of Ffrangcon's style—complaining of the use of such adjectives as 'psychic' and 'architectonic' in the definition of that type of thought which Ffrangcon insisted should inspire a singer's work. To this review he replied in a letter to the editor composed entirely of words of one syllable, of which the following is an extract:

> Sir, I come of that wild race men call the Welsh, from out the far side of the great long Dyke; and now for my sad sins do dwell in this strange land where they who speak it know not how to grasp all that which one may say to them in their own tongue. I fain would seek the cause of things so strange; but depths like this no man can plumb! My own wild folk—though some of them may break, not heart, but rocks, and some are black with grime of coal but not with ink of spite, nor do they dive for wit in one small pot of ink—yet they are keen, and wield great words and small. . . . All minds have this gift, would they but use it, aye, to deal with words of more than one foot long. But lo, the sage who sits and waits your nod to speak, now soft now hard words, of the men who are so mad that they make books which they who read may run, is wrath that I use words too long and thoughts that are too dark for him. Two words are these: psy-chic and arch-i-tec-ton-ic. They mean, the first: with soul in it; the next: with some true sense in it. Your sage doth seem to be too frail and short of *soul* and eke of *sense*. . . . My words are small and all of one short span and yet that

which they say, I rede, is plain. All this—from him who wrote of song that yet may be.

To offset this charge of obscurity came a letter and enclosure from his publishers on November 9th: '. . . perhaps nothing will please you more than a letter I now send you from a working-man in St. Albans who is paying for your book in instalments. It is the first book which has ever been ordered from me in this manner.'

In a lecture given by Sir Edward Elgar in Birmingham (No. IV, 'English Executants') shortly after the publication of *The Singing of the Future*, he said:

A book has been written by Ffrangcon-Davies, a thoughtful book as far removed from ordinary dry-as-dust tuition as it is possible to conceive, on the art of singing. I advise you to read it. . . . Our singers are by critics often lectured for their want of brains; they must *think*. Well, here is something for them to think over, and it cannot but help them to a better understanding of their art and their responsibilities.

# V

NEARLY TWENTY YEARS have passed since my father's death and thirty since he walked normally as a man among men. The last years of his life—owing to his prolonged illness—were shrouded in a gloom which, terrible though it was for himself and his family, must for his friends have been quite overshadowed by the greater gloom of the World War. Yet the memory of him lives.

If it were possible to lay a finger on the secret of his ability to make and keep friends, it lay in his utter sincerity. Whole-hearted in his distinctions between black and white, to him the little things were always little and the big things big. Impatient of the second-rate, his patience with genuine effort was boundless. Exacting, he was generous; serious, he had a childlike gaiety; like all strong men, he could be considerate and ruthless in extremes. Yet his loyalties never wavered.

How highly Ffrangcon valued not only his friends but his acquaintances is shown in the care with which he treasured innumerable letters and items of news; it is largely from his scrap-book that this chapter is drawn. In order to prevent it from becoming a mere rehearsal of names—the last thing he himself would have tolerated— I have mentioned in an earlier chapter the contacts in America which he so much prized, and have also given a place apart, as it deserves, to the unending kindness of

Madame Clara Novello Davies and her husband from the beginning to the end of his career.

Among his early friendships none was more precious to him than Ellen Terry's—however slender it may have been. It was to her he turned in the earliest days for advice as to how he should approach the management for his first contact with the British opera. Her reply is full of pithy counsel. A later letter, dated April 29th, 1890, reads:

DEAR MR. DAVIES,

Here's a box for Monday—our dullest night, but never mind! On no night could *The Dead Heart* be called a cheerful play! If you have not seen it, you will find it, I think, a 'very good song very well sung,' but it's a song without words—a fine theme but not a line of literature. Miss Harries tells me you are always singing now. Do you love it? I hope so.

With very kind remembrances,

Yours sincerely,

ELLEN TERRY.

The charming little set of doll's tea-cups Ellen Terry gave to Gwen, my sister, and later her very kind encouragement of her professional work, is evidence that the friendliness endured.

My one personal recollection of this great lady dates from the war, when I was selling programmes at a charity concert in the Queen's Hall, at which many well-known people were present. Standing outside a door during the performance of one of the items on the programme, I was approached by an elderly, grey-haired woman, whose carriage and manner arrested my interest, and whom I immediately recognized as Ellen Terry. Searchingly she looked into my face and said: 'Who are you, child?' I told her. In an instant her arms were about me and she kissed me, saying: 'Oh, my dear, how much I loved your father!'

Friendly letters treasured from 1889 to 1896, and docketed in order of date, are from Augustus Mann, Sims Reeves, Paolo Tosti, Arthur Sullivan, Sir Henry Irving, Charles Hallé, George Henschel and Edward Lloyd.

In January 1900 a letter containing New Year greetings from Stanley Hawley ('May all the new days be better than all the old days') shows how little his friends saw of Ffrangcon during those strenuous years. 'I cannot tell you,' Mr. Hawley writes, 'what a delight the sign of your well-known handwriting gave me! I never knew where to address you. I heard of you one day as being in San Francisco, the next in "Thibet," the next God knows where; so I thought of sending you a letter addressed "D. Ff-D., Heaven." I also heard of your unexpected appearance at Pagani's one day. Why did you not send me a wire? I'll always join you when you alight in this country, if only for two minutes. What a gorgeous programme, the one you enclosed! And what a privilege for any German artist to hear you sing and take a lesson in what singing ought to be.'

But if his work kept him much away from England at that time, he was clearly enjoying new contacts. The position he held in Berlin, not only among Germans or amongst artists, but socially with his own country-men, is shown in the letter he received in March 1900 from Lord William Cornwallis West (then on a visit to his daughter, Princess Henry of Pless, in Berlin), who wrote discussing my father's forthcoming concert in that city and of the distinguished guests who were to be present there. Ffrangcon tremendously appreciated the interest thus shown in art generally, or in his work in particular, by men and women whose time he knew to be fully occupied with national and international duties, and he never failed to comment gratefully upon it.

Sir Hubert Parry, in 1901, in a letter which he signs 'very sincerely and gratefully yours,' wrote to my father: 'I shall never forget how completely your singing of *Saul's Dream*, at Birmingham, reached to the very highest ideal and desire I could have of its interpretation.' Sir Charles Stanford, discussing a concert programme, says, 'I have omitted *Prospice*, because two Stanford songs on a programme conducted by Stanford is too much; not from any lack of appreciation of your splendid singing of it.'

There is material and to spare amongst my father's treasures to build an estimate of the friendly relations which existed between himself and the great artists with whom he collaborated in the course of his career. Madame Adelina Patti gave him a diamond tiepin (which he in turn gave to his young friend Ivor Novello), and in later years, to commemorate their long association, she gave my father a very beautiful pearl, of which I am now the proud possessor. The letters of Madame Clara Butt, Sir Landon Ronald, Ben Davies, Granville Bantock, Mr. A. Randegger (with whom Ffrangcon coached on many occasions), have all survived the years; and every musician I have met who ever worked with my father has welcomed me for his sake.

I should like to quote from a letter in 1906 from Professor Sir Henry Jones, Professor of Moral Philosophy in the University of Glasgow, which must have pleased Ffrangcon coming from so rare a mind and distinguished a teacher:

God bless you for your kind heart! If letters like yours do not tighten one's grip of the sword, it means

that the virtue has oozed out of one's life. Its directness
and frankness are as evident as its generosity. I'll work
a little the harder yet, for your kind words. . . . Will
you, the first time you come to Glasgow, give me the
chance of being your host? I would fain believe that
your Master is also mine, and if we met we could talk
of the service, for it *is* moral, if it is real at all; and
whether it takes the form of literature or of song, it can
still be worship. . . . This old world, reeling on its
course, under its burden of sin and sorrow, still 'means
intensely and means good.' We'll go ahead, Mr. Davies,
and we'll arrive! May you be long strengthened to sing
the *meaning* of things and to declare the loving joy of
God in all His creatures.

In John Mahler's book, *Lead Thou*, printed for private
circulation in 1916, the author has some illuminating
things to say of his friend and teacher:

It was there (Leeds Musical Festival 1904) I caught
the first glimpse of the new world. I cannot now recall
any other item on the programme than a scene from *The
Mastersingers* in which D. Ffrangcon-Davies sang the
Hans Sachs part. There was a subtle something about his
singing and his whole personality that stirred me as I
had never been stirred by any singer, and that gave me
the sense of being indeed in the presence of a Master
Singer, and a master mind and spirit. . . . My desire
was to have a course of tuition from him—and I was
given an appointment. I began by singing to him half a
dozen songs from Schubert's *Winterreise*. He allowed me
to proceed with barely any interruption or comment
until I came to the last of my group, the 'Leiermann.'

He had only played a few bars for me when he turned round and said . . . 'Now will you start again and *give it me in your own way?*' I mention this as showing the extraordinary insight which enabled him to detect at a first meeting that my rendering of the song was a borrowed one, and because it was with him so vital and fundamental a principle in Art as in every phase and department of life: 'Give it in your own way.' His verdict on my singing and on the potentialities of my voice was encouraging, and it was arranged that I should come up to London roughly every month for three or four lessons on consecutive days. I soon found out that things spiritual entered very largely into all sides of his life, and by no means least into his song and his teaching of song. And I began to understand the quality and nature of that mysterious something which had so powerfully drawn me. In November 1907 . . . he was to sing the Christ in Elgar's Oratorio, *The Apostles*, at the Philharmonic Hall in Liverpool, and I felt I must be there. I saw him just before the performance and said, 'Well, Ffrangcon, I've come to hear you.' 'My dear man,' he replied, 'for God's sake get rid of the personal element or you'll lose the whole lesson of it.'

From Rutland Boughton, who worked with my father for several years, accompanying him, rehearsing in his studio for hours at a time, I have recently received a clear and vivid account of Ffrangcon's impersonal and infinitely patient approach to his work. Indeed, it speaks volumes for an artist if he can be—and can remain through the course of thirty years—a hero to his accompanist.

It was from Arthur Fagge that I first learned how Edward Elgar, hearing of Ffrangcon's illness, said: 'We shall not see his like again,' and to the end maintained his place had never been filled. Sir Henry J. Wood, with whom my father was associated throughout his entire career, endorsed that statement, when I quoted it to him, in a recent interview specially intended to discover whether the warm appreciation he expressed of the man and his work during Ffrangcon's lifetime had survived the years. 'Quite apart from the natural beauty of his voice, your father had brains,' Sir Henry said, 'and he used them. That was the supreme secret of his "difference." He had a deep religious fervour, a dramatic sense and he was not afraid to show the world what he thought and felt. *He was not Welsh for nothing!*'

As early as November 1899 Sir Henry wrote to Ffrangcon in Berlin to thank him, 'for all the trouble and pains you took to get your friends interested in our concert; we are indeed grateful. I am sure you were wise to rest after your fatiguing journeys; I am afraid we hurried you back to Berlin. How I wish I could attend some of your recitals—we both enjoyed your Lieder singing; it was a rare treat. Do come to London and sing at one of my Symphony Concerts—we do want a real dramatic Baritone in London badly,' and in June 1903 he wrote: 'Accept my sincerest thanks for agreeing to sing at six "Proms" . . . you did make a great impression on Saturday afternoon, saved the performance in fact, much love—always yours.' In 1904, inviting him to sing at the next season of Promenade Concerts, Sir Henry wrote: 'I do hope you can see your way to help me again with your indispensable services.'

A letter from Madame Olga Wood to my father in 1902 serves to refresh my memory of that gracious woman, whose early death was a sorrow to us all. I remember how she used to give us quantities of lovely ribbons for our dressing-up box, from the bouquets she received whenever she sang, and how proud we were to possess them.

It brings Ffrangcon very near to see so many of his friends still vigorously engaged in doing the work that he himself laid down long ago, and to remember that if his own life was short, yet 'art is long.'

I have reserved to the last my father's friendship with Sir Edward Elgar, because it was a thing apart in his life— a mountain-peak to which he never failed to lift his eyes and would not suffer to have brought down to the level of the everyday. In Edward Elgar Ffrangcon found a man who, like himself, had discovered the well of water which could wash away the dust of earthly things—so that with him he could speak of his disappointments. Here was a man who, no less than himself, reached up to the stars, and perhaps more often touched them; with him Ffrangcon could share his inspirations.

Mrs. Elgar Blake, daughter of the late Sir Edward Elgar, found among her father's papers some forty letters of Ffrangcon's, carefully preserved; these she has given me, and because they speak their own message I will add a selection of them here, gratefully acknowledging Mrs. Blake's permission to publish at the same time some of the letters from Sir Edward which I found in my father's collection.

LONDON.
*Sunday, 22nd June,* 1902.

MY DEAR ELGAR,

I am anxious to do what I can. My life has been a strange one and I may have learned something which may help the artist-student and perhaps may open the eyes of those who listen to us. It is so horrible to be regarded as a Canarybird in a cage!

You will know—without any disclaimer from me—that I do not imagine I have been born to set things right. I merely want to do what I can for the Art which I venture to hope I love strongly and cleanly—before I go hence and be no more seen.

I am,

Yours with true regard and respect,

DAVID FFRANGCON-DAVIES.

LONDON.

*Sunday*, 26*th October*, 1902.

MY DEAR ELGAR,

With all my heart, I congratulate you on the superbly strong impression you made on that mass of British humanity in Queen's Hall to-day. You stirred them all to genuine enthusiasm, and one felt that the heart of them beat in unison with your own.

Will you let me—with all diffidence—make a suggestion in regard to the great baritone solo. I felt impelled to make it after the Sheffield performance, but I refrained, until I had done it once more. I honestly believe I can make twice the effect if I may be allowed to take just a shade more time with the words, and to make the phrases a trifle broader.

I feel—all through—somehow that I have not quite enough time to get a grip of the words, and I failed to get the full effect both at Sheffield and Queen's Hall. I do not want of course to interfere with the rhythm—only to get more weight on the words and music. I throw myself on your forbearance if I am making too

32

bold a request. You will I know feel sure that I am only anxious to interpret you to the best of my ability.

My sincere greeting to Mrs. Elgar and yourself.

Yours always,

D. FFRANGCON-DAVIES.

(The above letter refers to Sir Edward Elgar's work, *The Dream of Gerontius*.)

LONDON.

*29th December*, 1902.

MY DEAR ELGAR,

The year is all but gone, and I cannot let it pass without saying to you that I owe you a great debt for the uplifting of my spirit through your work.

My heart is heavy for the death of my Father—a noble fighter and a true friend to art and to me. He died on December 9th. . . .

I am anxious to send a copy of *Gerontius* as a present to a New York friend—who would be deeply grateful and appreciative if you would write a line or two on the title page and sign it. Any general thought would be suitable—nothing personal. This lady is at the head of a Musical College in New York and is a great power for good. Will you write something if I send the copy down to you.

My greetings to Mrs. Elgar and you.

Yours ever,

D. FFRANGCON-DAVIES.

MALVERN.

*30th December*, 1902.

MY DEAR FFRANGCON-DAVIES,

Our deepest sympathy is with you—we read of your

great sorrow and you have been in our thoughts many times.

All good wishes for the New Year: we have not sent the usual greetings this year for the very prosaic reason that the printer disappointed us. Here is a tiny scrap, my first note (made probably on the golf links) on a sorry shred of paper and pasted into my note-book for the 'Angel of the Agony'—this trifle to stick in your book I send in lieu of a card.

Of course I'll gladly do anything possible to oblige you in the way of signing a copy of *Gerontius*—and much else besides when the time comes.

Our kindest regards.

> Yours ever,
> EDWARD ELGAR.

LONDON.
31st December, 1902.

MY DEAR ELGAR,

Your letter came, with healing in its wings. It was a gentle and a generous thought which resulted in my being the possessor of this tiny bit of paper—with marks on it—which mean, that there came to you from the Infinite a 'flash of the will that can.' I am indeed proud to have it and sacredly I cherish it.

Your sympathy and that of Mrs. Elgar is indeed precious. I become conscious with a start, constantly, and say—My father is dead. I cannot tell what he was to me, and the very last time I was with him—how he spoke of you! I can see the look which would have come into his face as he listened—had he ever heard it—to

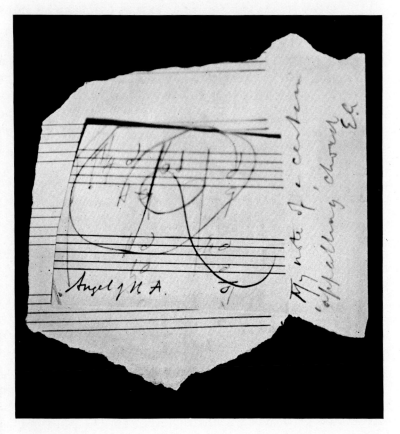

'*This trifle to stick in your book*'. *Elgar's note of '*a certain appalling chord,' for the* ANGEL OF THE AGONY

*Gerontius*. Thank you, dear friends. I am just off by the night train to Glasgow to sing in the *Messiah*.

A happy New Year to you both,

FFRANGCON.

LONDON.
*2nd January*, 1903.

MY DEAR ELGAR,

Your great kindness in writing within the cover of *Gerontius* for my friend in New York has given me and will give her infinite joy. The book is even now on its way to her.

I sang in *Messiah* in Glasgow yesterday. 'Twas heavy work and my heart aches physically. But give me time and I will bend my back with thankfulness to my burden once more.

My greetings to you both.

Ever gratefully,

FFRANGCON.

MALVERN.
*Good Friday*, 1903.

Jesu!

(Here follows a chord.)

MY DEAR FFRANGCON-DAVIES:

Very many thanks indeed for sending me the letter. You know how I feel about things! and it is good for me to read what people *really* feel. Press notices I never read on any account—I am told the work made an effect and my dear wife seems beaming with happiness. For

35

me all is closed—*closed up*—I want neither fame nor riches, so I don't trouble about print; so don't send me papers.

I hope the Westminster performance will come off and be good.

Kindest regards and again thanks.

Yours ever,

EDWARD ELGAR.

LONDON.

MY DEAR ELGAR,

One word of gratitude for your letter. It spurs one to know of one to whom so much of earth's kingdoms have been shown in a moment of time (it is not irreverent to imagine that in lesser degree and with lesser effect the Master's life is reproduced in mortals—who are nevertheless immortal), as has been the case with you and who renounces fame and name, honour and riches.

The letter I sent you was so beautiful that I could not but send it to you. As to ever daring to *think* even of sending you papers—I could not if I tried. You and your work are far beyond them to me. You saw in my last that I said my friend had—unasked—promised to send some papers to me but had not done so. I think I went on to say that *had* she done so I should certainly *not* have sent them on. It is only the real things that count.

Again thanking you,

I am,

Yours always,

D. FFRANGCON-DAVIES.

*Facsimile of first page of letter on page 35*

LONDON.
6th June, 1903.

DEAR MASTER MINE,

The work is nobler than ever—one is beginning to realize in some sort what there is to be done in it—what one must do and think and be, before one can hope to walk side by side with you on its heights. I saw new light—over and over again it flashed to-day. But, my dear friend, you demand the highest exposition, and we shall—we and our successors—have to begin to climb. For this we are your debtors.

I am just home from the Cathedral and it was all too much for me and my brain is tired. But let me make at least this clear, that you have the whole-hearted devotion and gratitude of a man who asks nothing better than to be a voice—to help in crying aloud the deep and unerring gospel which you preach.

Your servant,
FFRANGCON.

(The following four letters relate to Elgar's new work, *The Apostles*, and Ffrangcon's part in it of the Christ.)

LONDON.
6th March, 1903.

MY DEAR ELGAR,

I have been in deep waters—pneumonia for a fortnight. Writing from a gloomy standpoint—that of a bed-ridden man—you will forgive me for a weak letter. I want to make it clear to you that—if it be true that you meant to entrust me with your new work for the

Birmingham Festival (for which you have my deepest thanks) I am ready to hold myself entirely at the disposal of yourself and the Festival Committee.

Vert asked me to quote terms some time ago—and I with his approval made an ordinary Festival quotation. But—I told him if it were necessary, that I would make no point of mere money, though with the fearful losses I have met with lately, money is tight—naturally. If anything is said to you by the authorities will you let a sick man ease his mind by asking you to make it clear that I am entirely and gladly in their hands. All this sounds weak—but I have so often been made sport of and I at present fear everything; one's faith suffers from physical causes. I am fighting hard to be up and doing at Hanley.

In the silent night watches—I have heard with tears the 'Proficiscere'. I cannot write more; greet—please—Mrs. Elgar for me. You pardon me for writing.

Yours,

FFRANGCON.

TEMPLETON, MASS., U.S.A.
23rd July, 1903.

MY DEAR ELGAR,

Many days of drought and many days of tension in New York—made this morning all the fresher and the more grateful to tired senses and parched earth. On a circular turret, forming the corner of the verandah of this quaint old renewed house in New England—I sat with you and the *Apostles* this morning. Away in the distance are Monadnock and the Sunset Hills—with their ever-changing blues and mists—out of which they come to greet one on occasion—as they do to-day. Nearby the man is mowing the hay, and I hear the household at work.

But no rush and no rebellion—all is quiet and calm; and thought and I listen to your 'On the Wayside' and 'At Caesarea'. I am very glad of the 'Part.' It gives me a chance to grow slowly into it. They sent me Part I only! It wants the noblest art and the sternest self-repression—together with the power of seeing how He looked who came to bring a sword and who also knew to sorrow with the little family at Bethany and over the complex life of Jerusalem. That word 'Come!' to the faltering Peter is enormous! I feel sure that you are supremely happy over this your latest work.

I stand by and I uncover my head.

My greetings to Mrs. Elgar—and to you.

Yours always,

FFRANGCON.

MALVERN.
14th September, '03.

My DEAR FFRANGCON,

Please accept the poor photo of a fine picture: I know it will appeal to you, it is my ideal picture of the Lonely Christ as I have *tried* (and tried hard) to realize (musically for a few of us) the Character.

It is by a Russian artist and there is a history to the picture which I will tell you. I hope to be in town soon and of course will let you know.

Yours ever,

EDWARD ELGAR.

39

LONDON.

*16th September*, 1903.

MY DEAR ELGAR,

What shall I say first, what last, to make my gratitude clear for your thought of me! The thanks you will love best will be those of the soul, and—simply—the soul of me does thank you. The strong loneliness of the Saviour, and His manifest self-forgetfulness, are so plain to be seen. And your words, with the 'Beatitude' music, on the back of the photograph make me glad. I believe your realization of the Master will do a mighty work for the souls of men.

It will be good to see you and a sacred joy to sit down with you to the feast for the first time, when we try over my part. To Mrs. Elgar my greeting, please.

Yours,

FFRANGCON.

MALVERN.

*22nd October*, 1903.

MY DEAR FFRANGCON,

Can you come and see your friends on Saturday next till Monday? The prophet's chamber (a very small one) is at your service.

Yours ever,

EDWARD ELGAR.

LONDON.

*Thursday night.*

MY DEAR ELGAR,

You are very good and I hope to be with you on Saturday some time. I'll wire the time later. I am in York on Friday night and it is on the cards I may have

To my friend
& Ffrangcon Davies :

from Edward Elgar.

Sep: 1903

Blessed are they that mourn, for they shall be comforted.

*The Lonely Christ*

to sing at the London Pop. on Saturday, but I'll come down after, and have a peaceful Sunday—Sabbath Day—with you and Mrs. Elgar.

You have sent forth a Spirit through—by means of—*The Apostles* which will give this age pause.

Yours,

FFRANGCON.


P.S.—If I don't have to go to London on Saturday morning I'll come straight to Malvern from York.


LONDON.

MY DEAR ELGAR,

I am glad that the shelter of your roof has been mine. It was a time of supreme happiness to me. . . . Please commend me cordially to dear Mrs. Elgar, and convey my deep thanks to her for her kindness.

My reverence and my gratitude to you.

FFRANGCON.


LONDON.
*Sunday*, 24th *January*, '04.

MY DEAR ELGAR,

It is late and I am alone in my den, after a long and exciting day, singing, writing, discussing. A great man was here with us for about two hours to-day, Dr. Richter. After we had lunched we rehearsed. In the middle he stopped and spoke lovingly of England. In a moment he turned to you and evinced deep emotion while he discussed your work. I said no word, but fastened my eyes to his, and drank in the pleasuring homage which he paid to your strength. Such a mind as his, manifesting true appreciation of your spiritual and aesthetic gifts, was indeed something to wonder at. For he only loves giants nor does he speak readily, as you know. It all made me very happy. 'The greatest musician since Purcell in England.' 'Genius, not talent.' 'Individuality and loyalty to the truth as he sees it.' 'Always himself and always English, glorified by the Universe, in his compositions.' It is not only the keenest judges who acclaim you; the great heart of the world responds pulse for pulse to yours. . . .

The day has been heavy and I am weary. Let my very weariness prove to you the sincerity of the impulse to speak to you—mind to mind. The voice of God is our only music, we do not hear it well, when discordant voices break in upon us.

> *Oh, to hear*
> *God's voice plain as I heard it first, before*
> *They broke in with that laughter! I heard them*
> *Henceforth, not God!*
> *To Ancona—Greece—some isle!*
> *I wanted silence only—there is clay*
> *Everywhere. One may do whate'er one likes*
> *In Art—the only thing is, to make sure*
> *That one does like it—which takes pains to know.*
> 'PIPPA PASSES.'

You have been at pains, have agonized, have dwelt with your lonely Christ. Be comforted therefore and pity all shortcomings in all men. They—some of them—'do not know what they do.' That is all. Remember that your friend Ffrangcon is Welsh and forgive him accordingly.

Greet Mrs. Elgar right warmly.

GRAND HOTEL, MORECAMBE.
*29th April*, 1904.

DEAR MRS. FFRANGCON-DAVIES:

It was most kind of you to write and I looked forward to a quiet moment *here* to send you my thanks.

The quiet moment has come and with it Ffrangcon's letter in which he says I am not to trouble to write to you or to him. I was so glad to see you at the Albert Hall, having known and appreciated, in the real sense of the word, your husband so long and it somewhat made up for my misfortune in missing you when I have called at Acacia Road. I thank you for all the kind and good things you say. I can only answer 'We try.'

Believe me,
Yours very truly,
EDWARD ELGAR.

HEREFORD.
*7th July*, 1904.

DEAR FFRANGCON:

Many thanks for your kind congratulations. How I wish I could have been at York and heard you in the Minster. We are only partially in this house and the place is still in a muddle but very beautiful.

In great haste,
Yours ever,
EDWARD ELGAR.

(The following letter to Edward Elgar refers to a performance of *The Apostles* at the Covent Garden Festival, March 1905, conducted by Dr. Hans Richter.)

LONDON.
*March*, 1905.

. . . You have seen fruits of the travail of your soul and are satisfied. We too have shared your vision, and not one soul but is consciously or unconsciously the better for it. It may take some of us longer than others to fully realize what we have gained. For me, there is a fierce fight, ever waging, because I am keenly conscious of and sensitive to the spirit of worldliness which seethes around. I try hard to ignore it, but when at the most sacred moments it manifests itself, I fear that I am unable to stem the torrent of disaffection which rises against it. . . .

You, my dear Edward, have poured into my soul a balm yesterday and to-day which soothes my wounds. You do not cry aloud, nor is your voice heard in the market place. I will try and teach myself to follow in your footsteps. And yet—I have never fought for a personal point, though I find it hard to give way on a principle, even though there be a personal point attached to it. All through these performances at Covent Garden, whenever I was not singing and just as I got up to sing—I whispered to myself 'God, The Christ, and His servant Elgar's ideal of Him, are my sole concern.' . . . I have opened my soul to you, because it is a relief, and because I want you to see what you are doing for a man who can scarcely claim even that he sees through a glass darkly. It is half-past one in the morning and I am going to Leeds to-day—for *The Apostles*. I shall sleep more peacefully after writing to you.

Constructive power, one-ness succeeding many-ness,

a spirit which pierces between the marrow and the bone of every thought in the text, originality, strength, tenderness, these and many more, were my thoughts as I *lived* in every bar of *Gerontius* and *The Apostles* yesterday and to-day, thoughts upon the way in which you have done your work. Dr. Richter told me when he came to my house some time ago, in answer to my disclaimer of knowledge of musical composition, 'It is not necessary for you to know composition, in order to be able to give a just opinion.' And so I have ventured to say as much as I have said. Your own spirit—giant as it is —has been refreshed by the spirit of the giants. But, your face is always before me when I sing and your words and your music are *yours*, are *you*, every bar. And now for the days that are to come! Soar, dear Friend—from planet to planet; the universe is yours and God is your guide. We listen for your voice.

How happy Mrs. Elgar and you will be in your home, aye, and your sweet daughter.

Forgive my long letter and accept my soul's devotion.

FFRANGCON.

GLOUCESTER MUSICAL FESTIVAL, 1907.
13th September.

MY DEAR FFRANGCON,

Thanks from the deepest for all you have done for me and others this week and always. I had thought I should have seen you to-day but I find you have left.

Now comes a letter from Mainz begging me to use my influence to persuade you to go. You will have received a letter from them. I can only say that nothing could give me greater happiness than to know that you were singing my work in Germany but the fee they mention is of course impossible. So dear 'friend and brother,' only know that I should be happy whenever you sing for me and accept once more my thanks.

With love and I will add reverence for *your* art.

Yours ever,

EDWARD.

LONDON.

*September*, 1907.

MY DEAR EDWARD,

You are very good and kind. Our privileges are great. I offered to go and sing at your new series of concerts in Birmingham for nothing—for the Art's sake. The fixed fee of 'twenty guineas' I could not consider. The Mainz fee is, as you say, simply stupid. But 'thy money perish with thee!' So I address myself. I want to go— and *be* 'Peter' to them. And if I go, I go on the condition that I am not forced to tear out my voice to be heard. The modern accompaniment as it is played is lethal. Let the players 'listen to' the soloist, as you say in regard to the chorus. You are high and great and strong. Put your foot down, dear Edward, and fight, for the sake of others if not for your own.

Listen! I'd go to the end of the earth to serve you. You will realize my sincerity one day, my 'friend and brother.' I owe you love, and I'll pay you love. Your music is diviner and deeper every time I hear it. But 'The Spirit' must be over us all. 'The Kingdoms of this World' distract me at times.

Yours ever.

FFRANGCON.

P.S.—Remember: 'I was ever a fighter.' But I *can* love.

# VI

IT IS THROUGH his letters to my mother covering a period
of twenty years, and through the men and women who
were his friends, that I have learnt to know my father,
for my personal recollections of him are always of the
artist, absorbed in his work, aloof, austere. Of the sane
enthusiasms, the sweet naturalness, which charmed his
friends and lives to-day in their memory, Ffrangcon's
children learnt little, though the desire to know him as
he really was, to discover the secret of his vision and to
follow the trail he blazed, has been the strongest incentive
in my life and led me early to a careful study of the teaching contained in his book, which I found—and still find—
to be the highest authority.

Something in the sheer beauty of his voice beckoned me
in childhood, as in memory it holds me still; and it is
with reverence that I subscribe to the words written across
his well-used score of *The Dream of Gerontius* in Edward
Elgar's handwriting, and signed by him (at the Sheffield
Festival, 1902): 'For Ffrangcon-Davies, Deo Gratias.'

The first home I can remember was in Berlin. Our
brother Geoffrey was little more than a baby and even
Gwen and I were too young to take seriously to heart the
fact that our father's high sense of rectitude and idealism
was sometimes clouded; too young also to value the fact
that that sense, founded on the rock of a true religion,
emerged again and again, unshaken and unspoilt after each

darkening. 'Once a priest,' he said to his intimate friends, 'always a priest.'

During these years Ffrangcon was both enduring and achieving much. 'Your letter,' he writes to his wife from England,

was handed to me at lunch. I freely own that you have had and have much to try you. . . . I love you and I *am* sorry to make you suffer. I don't do it willingly, I assure you. Perhaps when I get more of what I deserve artistically, I shall have more to lay at your feet and to give you. It makes me *angry* to have to stint you in any way. A public man ought to be treated with great consideration.

Again, in a letter from America addressed to my mother in Berlin, Ffrangcon wrote:

I am considerably spent bodily, but strong mentally. I am quietly working on my book; it will be a solace to me in leisure hours for another year. . . . I am delighted to hear the babies are favourites: I don't see how they could fail to be, brought up as they are. All the news you give me of them is exceedingly welcome. Their education is the one great thing now. They will be enormously helped by German thoroughness and exactness. I see there is a tear blot on your letter, just where you are talking of 'marks'! Well, it may be that later we shall not care so much about money. Meanwhile a fine cheerful spirit works wonders. My Art is the tree, in the shade of which all I love may shelter securely. I have developed and grown prodigiously in the last three months and am doing fine work. . .

God bless you for your strength, virtue and motherliness.

Something of the 'prodigious growth' mentioned in that letter was recognized in 1901 when next my father sang in London. He was travelling almost continuously now, and felt the strain both physically and mentally; but he was also tasting the satisfaction that must come to every artist who finds himself able to serve more and more effectively the art he loves. His technique was by this time perfected and enabled him to achieve results which were all the more arresting because they served his ideals and never his personality.

As years of experience strengthened his faith in his original standards and method, and as each task was approached with greater authority, so his power of expression grew. And whatever he sang, in whatever language—from a florid Handelian aria, from the *Largo al Factotum*, the Prologue to *Pagliacci*, the *Flying Dutchman*, down to the *Bay of Biscay* and *Father O'Flynn*—every word was distinctly audible even in the farthest confines of the largest hall.

In spite of these achievements Ffrangcon was not a happy man! He loved and longed for his home, his wife, and his children. 'I am only supremely content when my wife and bairns are near and understand me,' he wrote to Nan; and again:

Your opening sentence is a little puzzling: '*over two weeks and no letter*.' No two weeks have passed without my writing—no one week. But you need not claim any monopoly of loneliness! If you could undertake my life for a month or so, you would, I fancy, be a little

E

more content than you are! I am at the limits of my endurance. . . . I am having a time of infinite drudgery and hard work. No, I do not touch stocks or gambling; I *sing* or *teach* for all the dollars I make. I am feeling very tired and worn and cannot be called upon for illimitable small nothings. So long as I feel you are all right and well—and the children—I address all my strength to the endless details of my career.

But of those nervous crises which now began to loom in our own home there is no shadow in any of the letters from the many friends in whose homes Ffrangcon was always a welcome guest. Mrs. Harriet Green, the wife of his friend, Dr. Green, in St. Louis, once wrote to my mother as follows, acknowledging

the delightful pictures of yourself and the three cherubs of children. It was touching and most beautiful to see your dear husband when the pictures were withdrawn from their envelopes . . . while we sat at the breakfast table. . . . I find, dear Mrs. Ffrangcon-Davies, that our husbands have many habits in common; they both like to smoke, they both like to tell stories, they both hate to go to bed at night, they both hate to get up in the morning! *My* dear cannot make three musical notes, albeit he has a musical voice in speaking; *your* dear could not utter one unmusical note, and his speaking voice is also musical. Each spirit is attuned to the best and highest note that the human spirit can reach—and each deserves all the love and tenderness we can give. We took your husband to our hearts and our home, not as a stranger, but as one who belonged to us. We hope we may one day see you face to face in the sweet

companionship of him whose absence (from you) has
brought to us renewed assurance in music through an
ideal spirit.

A letter from Ffrangcon accompanying Mrs. Green's
refers also to the photographs. 'Please tell the children
that I long for them every day. I have those pictures with
me. All my friends are delighted with them; Schumann-
Heink was wild about them.'

In September 1901 Ffrangcon places on record: 'I gave
a Travelling Recital here at Yaddo, Saratoga, last night
exemplifying the following countries: Wales, Scotland,
Ireland, England, France, Germany, Switzerland, Norway,
Russia, Turkey, Greece, Italy, Spain, Morocco and
America. I sang in eight different languages.' His friends
needed to be men and women of the broadest sympathies
and keenest perceptions to keep up with the boundless
energies and unflagging enthusiasms of such a man.

One such was Ordway Partridge, the sculptor, who
made a bust of my father. 'He got me in clay first and then
cast it in plaster; I think it very good.' 'Partridge is very
interesting,' says the next letter,

and a joy to me, and I sincerely hope he will be to
you, one day, when we can all be together . . . when
we can have our settled, quiet home-life and when the
turmoil is lulled to rest. The book gets on, but I don't
love it as my 'child.' I have the children born to me of
you, and they are more to me than anything. Life is
greater than Art. But my life must follow art even as
art must illume my life. Does Geoffrey learn his letters
yet? I fancy he would learn English in play, almost, with
Gwen and Marjorie; I am sorry the little woman cut

her foot so badly. . . I fancy the worst is over and your
reward will come. Nothing matters much but setting
one's teeth and working the day's work. . . It is the
people who live from within, outwards, and not the
people who live from without, inwards, who are happy.
Father is in Rhyl, recovering well; I want him to give
up his work. He could teach music to amuse himself.

Taid, my grandfather, lived until December 1902, and
his son's wishes for him were fulfilled.

A Press notice appearing in the *Magdeburg Zeitung*
gives a very vivid description of the impression made by
my father at this period of his career, and is particularly
interesting in the light of events which followed:

> David Ffrangcon-Davies—an artist who is an alto-
> gether unique phenomenon. It belongs as much to the
> psychologist as to the musician to explain the singularity
> of this gifted man. . . . He is a supreme master of the
> voice, and surely such a voice we shall rarely find. . . .
> What he sings is severely serious and moves in the
> sphere of exalted ideas; this serious view of life, through
> which every now and then rings the fine disdain of a
> harrowed soul, we shall not often note in a singer."

He was forty-five years old when this notice appeared.
What had life done to him, that through his serious view
of it should ring 'the fine disdain of a harrowed soul'?
It had offered him a compromise—and to a man of
Ffrangcon's idealism a lowering of the standard was inadmissible. He had refused to subordinate to mere academics
his sense of art, or barter for mere popularity and com-
mercialism his awareness of the artist's mission. He asked

nothing better than to give life of his best. But sanctuary a man must have!

Weakened by the perpetual struggle, Ffrangcon began to fear his recourse to alcohol to sustain him, and there came a moment when, in all good faith, Nan and he decided to try the effect of hypnotic treatment. Many of their closest friends in Berlin were infected by this fashionable craze and urged my parents to follow it, little dreaming how devastating this deviation from the normal would prove to a man of Ffrangcon's inheritance and character.

Acting on the advice of a doctor, they addressed themselves to a well-known hypnotist, and treatment was begun. Grievous though the effect of this treatment was upon my father, and terrible the havoc it wrought in all our lives, in fairness it should be said that, after the suggestion of personal mastery had been implanted (so that he never again touched alcohol), he was instructed to return at the end of a year for further treatment. It is idle now to speculate upon what might have been the result— exchanging for some other idea the obsession of domination which, from now onward, took periodically the place of the old craving; for he never underwent this second treatment.

Returning to England, we settled in London in circumstances and surroundings which, at their face value, should have been entirely comfortable for my mother and happy for us all. Nan and he furnished the house together with great care and a keen interest in every detail, and it was perhaps the only time in his life that he gave himself over to the luxury of indulging thus his love of beauty; and he never ceased to appreciate the result.

Here in 1904 he began his duties as a teacher of singing at the Royal Academy of Music. The following year his book was published, the writing of which had occupied all his happiest and freest moments. How often I have wished that in our childhood we had known more of the perfect love which casts out fear! Why could we not have learnt to laugh and scold and tease our father, as others did! The widow of the Rev. John Edwardes Evans, my father's oldest and most intimate friend, told me of an occasion when Ffrangcon, staying at their vicarage in Cheshire, so exasperated her by getting the better of some futile argument that she sent the great man up to his room with no more ado than if he had been an unmanageable schoolboy. And, quite simply, he obeyed her, and as naturally was restored to grace.

He loved the genuine and simple things of life; who better than his children could have shared them with him? We were healthy, normal and cheerful, and we were all musical. In Gwen, his eldest, he might have found a fascinating companion; she was early drawn to the things that he loved best; long before I could understand it, he must have recognized the promise of her artistic talent.

My cherished memories of my father are all of his singing, and especially in the performance of Elgar's *Apostles*, in which he took the part of the Christ, and of *The Dream of Gerontius*, where all the melting loveliness of his voice was needed in those words of Cardinal Newman's poem:

*Jesu, by that shudd'ring dread which fell on Thee;*
*Jesu, by that cold dismay which sickened Thee;*
*Jesu, by that pang of heart which thrill'd in Thee . . .*
*Jesu, spare these souls which are so dear to Thee,*
*Souls who in prison, calm and patient wait for Thee;*
*Hasten, Lord, their hour, and bid them come to Thee,*
*Jesu, spare these souls which are so dear to Thee.*

He seemed transfigured when he sang, and all my childish dread of him, as of a lonely giant inhabiting some cold strange universe, was dispelled, so that he became by some mysterious process a being at once sublime and entirely natural.

Entirely natural he was too in his moments of puckish fun, as when he would sing *Simon the Cellarer* so convincingly that I never doubted my own chubby person was this same Dame Margery, and considered myself hopelessly and permanently on the shelf when, after chuckling his way through the song, he reached its final shout, 'What! Marry old Margery? No, no, no!'

Few indeed were his light-hearted moments. He regarded art as a redemptive mission, nor is he the first great singer in history to hold that view and claim a place for it in the world's reckoning. Is not that greater David, the psalmist of Israel, remembered for the songs he sang, the works he did, the love that he inspired, rather than for the frailties of his temperament?

# VII

IN GAINING A clearer estimate of the last ten years of my father's life, I have been driven first to overcome a horror of the fact that he spent the greater part of those years in a mental home; next, to regard that home as a sanctuary which became to him—in the true Greek meaning of the word Asylum—a place inviolable; and lastly, to appreciate that without the sublimating process of that isolation his human life would have been robbed of its crowning experience.

Ffrangcon had preached the gospel, had sung his song, and had written his book all on the theme of the quickening Spirit and subordinate flesh, the Will done not only in heaven but on earth. He believed that good and joy and harmony have the mastery over evil and discord and sorrow. Now the one thing that remained to him was to prove it.

Singing, teaching, writing, warring, he drove himself mercilessly to work sixteen, eighteen, sometimes twenty hours a day. Well might he have said in Chesterton's beautiful words:

> So, with the wan waste grasses on my spear,
> I ride forever, seeking after God;
> My hair grows whiter than my thistle plume,
> And all my limbs are loose, but in my eyes
> The star of an unconquerable praise;

*For in my soul one hope forever sings,*
*That at the next white corner of a road*
*My eyes may look on Him.*

Youth has its defences, and our own lives were obscured
by this impending tragedy but not crushed by it; it was
on my mother that Ffrangcon's torment of mind fell most
heavily. Looking back upon it, as through the far end of a
telescope, I can see only isolated pictures, pitiful glimpses
of what must have been a continuous struggle in the home;
almost photographically, incidents come to mind whose
significance I was too young to understand but which at
the time united to impart to each of us a haunting fear.
When the first autumn gales sweep through the late
summer, and the mists hint that the crown of the year is
past, I remember Ffrangcon, my father, whose own
summer prime was prematurely swept by tempest and
whose bleak November claimed him all too soon!

The climax was inevitable. Late in 1907 in the Albert
Hall he sang with indescribable beauty Wotan's Abschied,
and ended with Gounod's setting of 'There is a green hill
far away.' Round after round of applause recalled him to
the platform, but after delivering the sacred message of
that hymn he refused to sing again. This was his last public
appearance for eleven years. A specialist diagnosed
Ffrangcon's mental state, and as a result he was placed in
Bethlem Hospital, where the full force of that congestion
of the brain brought on by years of tension and overwork
spent itself with gradually abating fury.

His illness, though not unexpected, had taken a far more
serious form than any could have anticipated. Yet the
storm died down at last, and as it passed Ffrangcon's
thought and longing turned towards his home. It is upon

that time I find it hardest to dwell. A truly sympathetic understanding of the situation is expressed in a letter Mrs. Harriet Green wrote from America to Nan:

> You are a marvel of faith and courage to have seen so much, endured so much, and known when the hour had struck. But how unspeakable the agony that envelops *him*, when he pleads to be taken home and is restrained. May God show him mercy and take this shipwrecked soul to His arms and give him the joy of rest. . . . Most of the songs Ffrangcon sang will ring in our ears forever. Oh the cruelty of stifling such powers! I feel as if I *must* find some means to rescue so great a light. Alas, alas, it seems a hideous nightmare, and I find myself trying to rouse from the terror in which I am groping.

In June 1908 Ffrangcon's doctors decided that he should return home on a visit, and his reactions be watched. It was then he awakened to the full significance of what life had done to him; he was a stranger in the home he loved! He needed care, quiet, and patient understanding. Where could he claim them?

Ffrangcon had his decision to make and he made it: he returned of his own choice to Bethlem Hospital and continued his struggle alone. His soul said with Gerontius:

> *Take me away, and in the lowest deep—*
> *There let me be,*
> *And there in hope the lone night watches keep*
> *Told out for me.*
> *There, motionless and happy in my pain,*
> *Lone, not forlorn,*

*There will I sing my sad perpetual strain,*
  *Until the morn.*
*There will I sing and soothe my stricken breast,*
  *Which ne'er can cease*
*To throb, and pine, and languish till possesst*
  *Of its Sole Peace.*

I remember that at some time during these dark years, and because of them, I wrote the only essay at school for which I ever received full marks. The subject set was, 'To prove the fallacy of the statement: "It is never too late to mend."' An instinctive and unquestioning protest arose in me and I wrote a composition of which every word escapes me now except the lines from Robert Browning's *Abt Vogler*, with which I closed it:

*There shall never be one lost good! What was, shall live as*
  *before.*
*The evil is null, is nought, is silence implying sound;*
*What was good shall be good, with, for evil, so much good*
  *more;*
  *On the earth the broken arcs; in the heaven, a perfect*
  *round.*

However much had already been achieved by the unsparing efforts of friends to rouse, to help, encourage and strengthen him, it was only after the tragedy of the war had broken loose over the world that he gradually awakened from his stupor. Here was a greater grief than his own, a deeper need and darker horror. The habit of self-forgetfulness and service slowly stirred, and with it the certainty returned at last that 'if with all your hearts ye truly seek Me, Ye shall ever surely find Me.' The hypnotic suggestion had burned itself out and Ffrangcon's healing—so long despaired of—had begun. He grew more robust, was able to go about a little, until slowly the hope dawned that he might yet resume his normal place amongst his fellow-men.

In May 1916 he began to write to his closest friends of his desire to use his talents once again in the service of mankind; invitations flowed in and he spent many happy days up and down the country visiting old haunts, courageously taking his first lonely forward steps, and then returning quietly to Bethlem, which remained his home to the last.

He received many splendid letters from old friends and kept them all; one from Ben Davies in 1916, giving him affectionate encouragement as to how, at this juncture, he might begin again to use the voice which had been silent for nine years. Granville Bantock, hearing of his return to health, wrote: 'May your second marriage with Life prove all that your friends and you could wish for.' John Mahler's letters are here; Arthur Fagge's also, written in Y.M.C.A. huts and telling of his life in France, and one from the Bishop of London to wish him 'Godspeed in your new life of service for Him.'

Our beloved young brother, Geoffrey, our parents' only son, was killed at the front. 'My dear little Gwen and Marjorie,' my father wrote to us after the sad visit we paid him at Bethlem on this occasion, 'I was very glad to see you both yesterday and to talk of our dear lad. . . .' Two young nephews, Harold Daniels and Jack Williams, almost as dear to him as his own children, were also destroyed in this vaster insanity of the world!

Of the beauty of his voice at the last his friends still speak, and it is true to say that it achieved a quality unknown before. A complete change seemed to come over him also; he was at peace with himself and with the world; he had found, and he had granted, forgiveness. Now his serenity fell like a benediction on the place which once was Bedlam.

The last letters which passed between Sir Edward Elgar and himself evidence the release which he had found:

LONDON.

*1st May.*

DEAREST FFRANGCON:

Your letter gave me the greatest joy, but, dear friend, I have been really ill with the Influenza, better last Tuesday but since then bad again, so you must forgive me for delaying even for a day my reply. After all, this is not an answer to your letter—that must wait until I return from Leeds.

I am sending you the two new things. Binyon's words are very fine and I will send the tickets soon. I shall hope to see you as soon as I am again settled.

Love to you,

Yours ever,

EDWARD ELGAR.

HAMPSTEAD GARDEN SUBURB.

*9th May.*

MY DEAR ELGAR;

'How still it is!'

I write at midnight in my wife's little flat, she has gone to rest, and I am now alone with the memories of to-night's wonderful experience. Surely, my dear Friend, surely the Master was 'Not very far' from you

when you poured your soul into the pages which tell
so poignant a tale of a soul in travail. *Gerontius* is a
burning bush, and its fire is very fierce and devouring
to all things that are alien to its inward spirit. Many
people have gone to their homes the purer for having
been under your influence to-night. I can speak very
certainly of the effect on two present. My wife, who
has been very sorely tried for many years, showed by
her keen following of the score the joy she felt at
hearing so great a performance of a work she has heard
on many occasions, and experienced a refreshment the
like of which she cannot call to mind. And this, in face
of our boy Geoffrey's death at the front. He sleeps in
a quiet Churchyard in Flanders. You can well imagine
how we listened to the music of *For the Fallen*. 'We
will remember them,' when 'They went with songs to
battle.' Geoffrey by all accounts was the singing and
the merry one of his group, many of his comrades bore
testimony of this to his Mother.

My love to you,

Ever yours,

FFRANGCON.

C/o CEDRIC CHIVERS, ESQ., J.P.

9 COMBE PARK, BATH.

MY DEAR ELGAR,

I am just back in the house from a sort of bungalow
in the grounds, where I sang 'By the Wayside' from
*The Apostles*. I'd gone down there with your *Apostles*
under my arm to commune with you and the work.
But there was a worn war-worker, a nurse engaged on
night duty there, resting a bit before going home to
bed. (My host places his house, home and all he has at

the disposal of these good souls.) This lady loves your music and heard *The Kingdom* in Birmingham, but never *The Apostles* so I just sat down and sang the Beatitudes, and fitted in all the other parts, Mary, John, Peter, Judas and chorus, as best I could.

I am in full command of voice and technic and can do now what I used to try and dream of doing in the old days. You can scarcely believe it, but it *is* so. I'm down on a visit here—in an ideal home surrounded by love, and care. I sang songs and read Browning to about sixty nurses and war workers the other evening. I've got your *To Women* and *For the Fallen* with your inscription on 'em to me down with me.

I trust you are well again.

My love to you,

Yours ever,

FFRANGCON.


In connection with this visit to Bath, Mr. John Hatton wrote to me of 'a vivid recollection' of my father's visit.

Your Father then stayed with Alderman Cedric Chivers, who at that time and during several subsequent years was Mayor of Bath, a great and unusual host, and a patron of the arts. Your Father sang at the Pump Room—many songs I think, but I can only remember (and that very clearly) one beginning 'Into the Woods the Master went.' His singing of this song was beautiful and moving, but he was very exhausted after, and the concert had to be curtailed. My other recollection is that we were gathered in a large garden room—a sort of music room at the bottom of the garden which was known as 'The Quiet.' There your Father read Browning to us with a fire—and a gentleness—which moved us all. I have never heard Browning so beautifully read. But your Father's body seemed so frail that what one felt must be a great emotional strain seemed almost alarming. All this has remained clearly in my mind.

The song referred to is George W. Chadwick's setting of Sidney Lanier's poem, *A Ballad of Trees and the Master*, which was dedicated to my father, and contains the verse:

> *Into the woods my Master went,*
> *Clean forspent, forspent.*
> *Into the woods my Master came*
> *Forspent with love and shame.*
> *But the olives, they were not blind to Him,*
> *The little gray leaves were kind to Him,*
> *The thorn-tree had a mind to Him*
> *When into the woods He came.*

On his return from Bath to Bethlem Hospital, Ffrangcon was not well. He went about as usual, unwilling to give trouble, but after an attack of faintness the doctor persuaded him to go to bed. Next morning he insisted upon getting up, but the effort proved too much, and before help could reach him, he died—April 13th, 1918—at the age of sixty-two, alone in that small room where he had fought his long and valiant fight.

Ezekiel the prophet wrote of the world's blindness:

And lo, thou art to them as a very lovely song of one that hath a pleasant voice and can play well on an instrument: for they hear thy words but they do them not. And when this cometh to pass (lo, it will come) then shall they know that a prophet hath been among them.

The hills and valleys of Wales are still as magical in their loveliness, with the same changing lights and shades on the hillsides. Wild roses bloom down Conway lanes and the brook still sings under the grey slab that spans it on the steep mountain path. The Same who painted Sharon's rose still tints the valley blooms. Along the shore the waves beat in irregular monotone. The great seas surge beyond!

I thank you, David, my father, for your song.

# PART TWO

*The Singing of the Future*

*by*

DAVID FFRANGCON-DAVIES
MA., OXON

*To the memory of*

MY FATHER AND MOTHER,
DAFYDD AND GWEN

# PREFACE

*by the late Sir Edward Elgar, Bart., Mus.Doc.*

'THE SOUL WHICH has seen most of truth shall come to the birth as a philosopher, or artist, or some musical and loving nature.' I do not now follow Socrates into his subsequent divisions; for the moment it is enough that, as one who 'has seen most of truth,' he has included the Musician: and in this rich-sounding word I include all —composers, executants and critics alike—who labour, not for any selfish ends, but for the good of the art of music.

But musicians have not always shown to the world, when their works have come to the birth, that they have seen the most of truth. The art easily lends itself to make passing amusement for the frivolous and the unthinking; in this there is nothing to deplore: we should rather rejoice in knowing that music can be an amusement, for it in itself is never ignoble; this it can only be when allied to unworthy words or to degrading spectacle. The many-sidedness of an art is a chief joy to its possessors, but the ineptitudes, and worse, of the creators of the material on which executants and critics live, have too frequently tended to degrade the two last-named in the exercise of their duties in their branches of the complete art. But with composers and critics and instrumental executants we need not now concern ourselves; although it may be profitably read by all musicians, this book is mainly for singers. I will add, for all singers; certainly

71

for all those proposing to sing, and certainly for many who have already embarked upon their professional careers.

With the march of time, and with it the improvement of musical education, a new desire has possessed us—the desire to *understand*. The desire has brought with it the interpreters we need. True, they are few in number and their array is meagre compared with the ample numbers and amiable affluence of the popular vocalists; but those who have 'the most of truth' are with us all the same, working, striving, and above all singing. Where in former days the vocalist entered upon his task with a light-hearted assurance that all the old 'points' would meet with un-questioning acceptance, the singer of the present day has to think as behoves a responsible artist. In circles of lesser value the modern ballad, with its unanalysable inanities, is still accepted as a recognizable form of art, but our better singers—our real interpreters and our teachers—have long ceased to affront their own intelligence by presenting the rubbish demanded by the uneducated for their pleasant degradation.

This book is a serious appeal to the singer, especially to the English-speaking singer, and I welcome it and hope for much real and lasting good from its dissemination. Written with complete knowledge by a singer who is also an artist, it forms a worthy portion, or it may be at this date a commencement, of that long-desired new edifice of English music which will some day be raised by those, and by those only, who have seen the 'most of truth.'

EDWARD ELGAR

*Hereford*
*December 1904*

# INTRODUCTION

THIS BOOK IS MEANT, not only for singers, but for all who are interested and concerned in the subject of speech or song—preachers, readers, pleaders, lecturers, reciters (with or without music) and actors—all of whom do their best work when they employ their best selves upon the best products of the best poets, dramatists and musicians. Our book also deals with the subject of daily speech, which is in truth the foundation of all artistic and, in the good sense, utilitarian utterance. He who *talks* best will, other things being equal, read, plead, recite, preach, lecture, sing and act best.

Aristotle defines Happiness as the state of 'A Soul at work in accordance with supreme virtue in a complete life.'

The good artist fulfils the conditions of this definition; and the good artist is the happy one.

D. FF.-D.

*London*
*Christmas Eve, 1904*

# I

## WHAT IS SINGING?

> *Lenzes Gebot, die süsse Noth*
> *Die legt es ihm in die Brust,*
> *Nun sang er wie er musst,*
> Und wie er musst, so konnt er's,
> *Das merkt ich ganz besonders.*
> HANS SACHS (*Die Meistersinger*).

WHAT IS SINGING? A full study of the voice would demand very accurate thinking and wide culture—results of excursions into fields of psychic, no less than physical, activity. Music and singing are a united territory, ruled over by intellect and soul, and reached by way of the senses. To combine healthy metaphysical insight and scientific accuracy in one pronouncement on vocal art would appear to be a rare achievement. Even when men like Ruskin, Emerson and Tolstoi have turned aside to discuss musical questions generally, their lack of precise musical knowledge has somewhat weakened their arguments. Again, composers too often seem to think that vocal art is an affair beyond their comprehension, that singing is a monopoly, and that it can never be anything else. They permit statements—the most absurd—to pass unchallenged, as though voice-production were a science which need not, like other sciences, abide by intelligent, artistic and progressive judgment. Plenary inspiration is claimed in regard to this science, tone is worshipped as a fetich, and confusion of doctrine prevails. When a composer's intelligence is startled by some extraordinarily extravagant dogma in the voice-producer's creed, he usually beats a hasty retreat.

Now voice and the singing instinct—regarded from the physical point of view—are comparatively scarce. But they are plentiful enough (if men gave greater heed to their psychic powers) to supply us with a far larger number of lasting and suggestive types of singers than we now possess. The singing instinct is more general, and musical ability more latently plentiful, than many of us imagine, as witness the behaviour of an audience under the influence of a Reeves or a Joachim. The germ is there; the step between appreciation and performance is not insurmountable; and as musical appreciation is more general than is usually supposed, so also is vocal power. Given a fairly keen sense of pitch and rhythm, in other words modest musical intuition and capacity for work, singing becomes a mere matter of practical development under the guidance of linguistic and imaginative thought.

The alleged fact that 'the world has always been ruled by the emotions' is no argument for continuing the sovereignty; especially as the word 'emotion' means so little to the average man. Sensuous frenzy and nervous excitement are very necessary in their place, but they are not the whole of art; nor is hypnotic vocal power the whole of singing—which must be histrionic, pictorial, plastic, as well as temperamental. If a life of varied experience has made the elements necessary for a singer's equipment fairly clear, in this book will be found some results of mental struggles undergone in the endeavour to find such a voice as would reflect the mind in its workings. The period of probation has lasted some seventeen years, and the growth of ideas has been slow. The manner in which these have been presented here may seem somewhat emphatic; if so, the writer trusts he may be forgiven. We all find it difficult to detach ourselves from our age and are therefore, when disposed to disagree, not over-easily convinced. Some emphasis, accordingly, a man must have.

It has been said that 'singing is a sustained talking on a tune.' This is a commendably plain statement; its value would have been increased had the author supplemented it by others suggestive of the poet, the philosopher and the artist. The ground is overrun by empiric theories, and too much of that which men say of voice culture is indefinite. How often the principle which underlies technique is lost in a multiplicity of details; and how seldom we are favoured with an all-embracing law which we can seize upon and carry about with us! Singing-primers, with their scales and exercises, fail to realize the value of organic principles tending to promote safe growth. Scales, like razors, are useful to those who can handle them; but in inexperienced hands they are dangerous. 'Singing is a sustained talking on a tune' helps the student to a clear view at the start. Keeping this in mind, he gives a simple and fairly convincing reading of a song. This type of singing has its value; its fault is amateurishness. But it not infrequently happens that amateurs can give a juster reading of a piece of vocal music than many a professional. A cultured amateur will often, with a voice of limited quantity, give a better balanced reading of the text.

Plenitude of voice does not always ensure plenitude of brains; it would even appear that the possession of the former tends to minimize the desire for the cultivation of the latter. When to the possession of a large and telling organ a fair amount of intelligence is added, and when moreover the sensuously pathetic appeal is present in the voice, the result is that a class of singing finds a vogue similar to that of ballad-singers. They 'talk on a tune' and so get at the hearts of their audience—whatever may be said of their brains. Yet, while exponents of this school go far, they do not go far enough. *They lack the sustaining line which appears only when unity of impression succeeds diversity of expression*, that is, when one whole picture takes the place of a series of sketches, or—one had almost said —splashes of colour.

What, then, is singing? For the seeker after artistic truth it is eminently wise and scientific to discover the highest pronouncements of the highest representative groups of human beings, so that he may enrich his own with the views of those who have touched high-water mark in the world's achievements. Prophets—men who love truth—are a necessity in art as in religion; they are also inevitable. The earnest student will not bow to popular judgments. If it be conceded that the highest ideals finally triumph in public estimation, yet the time taken by the public to realize the greatness of objective art emphasizes the zeal and educative power of individual performers rather than the innate perspicacity of the masses.

At the outset the student is stirred by the singing instinct to deal with the product of poets and musicians, men of cunning in the use of language and sound, some ancient, some modern. With the survival of the musical treasures of the past there has also come down to us a certain spirit in which they are to be approached, which arises out of the poetic and musical knowledge acquired by mankind. The singer must therefore seek to convey the creations of genius in such a way that the listener is enabled to hear and feel, fundamentally, what author and composer felt when placing their creations on record. This is an unvarying canon of interpretation. If then he attain to a fairly just combination, the amalgamated result of text and music in accord with the principles of literary and musical art, he may be said to have arrived at the goal of his endeavours: for this, in a broad sense, is 'singing.'

Guided therefore by mankind's culminative methods in pursuit of knowledge and its fruits, and by the results of those methods, we recognize as natural elements in music and singing:

(a) The poet's power seen in choice and handling of subject, and proved by the form of the text.

(b) The musician's power seen in choice and treatment of poet's text, and proved by the music's artistic fitness.

(c) The singer's power seen in his full sympathy with the subjects, methods and aims of various schools of poets and musicians, and proved by his progressive style.

These are the essence, the 'ego,' of singing, and may be said to be the things which tend to make the singer's art what it ought to be. On the other hand, there are things which tend to make it what it ought not to be. Some would make singing all tears; others, all smiles; some would have it all hypnotism; others, all intellect.

Now a false note is struck when a teacher's standpoint is the importation of the tear into the voice. The tyranny of those tears—and their morbid and lachrymose objects— would soon convert the sturdy and wholesome into the invertebrate and atrophied. But there may be a reason for the existence of such a school in the fact that tears (re-pressed) are a marketable commodity with those who cater for public entertainment! Others again insist upon a singer's looks when singing. Entertainment promoters make a great point of a 'nice appearance.' If instead we depend on the evolution of our character to manage the look on our face, we shall have some nature in it, as well as in the voice, and not the grin and mimetic note of our simian ancestor. Possessors of telling voices and engaging personalities are apt to depend on these entirely; while those who have a strong intellectual bent use it to the exclusion of all legitimate, personally hypnotic beauty or charm of voice. There cannot be any doubt that it is a prodigious error to take one fixed idea and to make that a basis for training. He who makes his voice the tool of any one sentiment (even though that sentiment be a safe investment) commits a crime against his voice, his character, and against nature.

Singers classify themselves according to supposed limitations; each finds his *métier* and lives up to and on it. Any singer of ordinary physique and mind should be able to delineate clearly any character. 'Such and such a rôle does not suit me,' is a statement one often hears. It is marked by indolence and apathy; for any rôle within a singer's vocal range should suit an artist. To some of us, at all events, it is clear that varied and even universal expression is the only kind of work to which any person of sense would care to devote his life. *Bel-canto* (of which we read so much) meant and means versatility of tone; if a man wish to be called an artist, his voice must become the instrument of intelligent imagination. Perhaps there would be fewer cases of vocal-specializing if the modern craze for voice-production could be reduced. This wondrous pursuit is, as things stand, a notable instance of putting the cart before the horse. Voices are produced and placed in such wise that pupils are trained to 'vocalize' (to use technical jargon) the words; that is to say, they are taught to make a sound which is indeed something like, but is not, the word in its purity. Tone or sound is what the average student seeks, *ab initio*, and not verbal purity. Hence the monotony of modern singing. This process of 'placing voices' results too often in their being put on the shelf, where they are indeed useless. When one hears an average singer in one rôle, one hears him in all. Many modern singers do not characterize. This charge would be inadmissible if they breathed properly and spoke the words with correct atmosphere; nor would it be possible in such a case to accuse them of pretentious or fictitious pronunciation and expression.

Our position is this: *voice must grow out of language and singers must begin their studentship by singing* THOUGHTS. The senses must not be allowed to tyrannize over the vocalists of the future, who will moreover show perfect correlative beauty and absolute agility of voice resulting from linguistic or, if you will, literary purity.

One sometimes fears that the term *bel-canto* is in some quarters perilously near *hocus pocus*; it is often used as though it were some preparation which singers apply to their voices—as ladies use unguents for their faces—to soften them. Broadly speaking, sensuous beauty or, as we are justified in calling it, 'prettiness,' is what people mean when they say that *bel-canto* had to do with 'beauty' of voice. It is because of this view that the principle of 'vocalizing' words, instead of musically saying them, crept in to the detriment of vocal art. This false position is due to the idea that the *arte del bel-canto* encouraged mere sensuous beauty of voice, rather than truth of expression. And yet it was a very seriously pursued study, this *arte del bel-canto.* Surely, on the face of it, *bel-cantists* must have concerned themselves with something higher than mere sensuous 'beauty of voice and vocal plastics.' Berlioz wittily alluded to the later and degenerate successors of true *bel-cantists* as 'performers on the larynx.'

Exact thinkers have ever looked with some amount of good-natured contempt upon musicians—upon vocalists especially, because of this very *pretty* madness. Singers and musicians are often held by clear-headed men of affairs to be specially emotionalized creatures, whose business is to affect the nerve-centres pleasantly. If someone will only give us a definition of beauty and a respectable theory of aesthetics, and then a digest of the social and religious thought-tendencies of the seventeenth and eighteenth centuries, we shall be able to talk rather more definitely about *bel-canto.*

There is one man who is sufficiently authoritative to help us, namely, Handel. The words of Robert Franz to Waldman (quoted by Mr. Finck in *Songs and Song Writers*) are definite: *'If any one understood the* bel-canto *of the Italians, it was Handel.'* Here, then, is firm earth. Another author, however, quotes a singer who has made himself famous as a 'colour' vocalist. This able actor-singer tells us (Apthorp's *Opera Past and Present*, pp. 184–5) that, 'in the days of the schools of the *arte del bel-canto*, the masters did not have to take "truth of expression" (*l'expression juste*) into account; for the singer was not required to render the sentiments of the *dramatis personae* with verisimilitude: all that was demanded of him was harmonious sounds, the *bel-canto.*' 'In other words,' this author goes on to say, 'beauty of vocal tone and beauty of musical plastics were the only recognized elements of emotional expression in singing, beyond that general fervour of delivery (*sic*) which may best be described as an absence of apathy. The emotions themselves were not to be differentiated, and the psychical character of the *dramatis personae* was not to be taken into account. All the singer had to do was to sing, and nothing else.'

If Handel had been privileged to read these strange pronouncements, one wonders what the result would have been—he could be fairly violent on occasion! The oratorio giant has suffered much from the assumption of those who have claimed that all that is demanded of Handelian singers is 'harmonious sounds and nothing else.' Imagine if you can the genial, poetic, imaginative and graphic Handel, who set to music most of the human emotions from the reflective 'Passion' to the thunderclap of the joyous 'Hallelujah' in *The Messiah*, and who certainly sounded some depths in emotional differentiation in *Samson*—imagine him being put off with pretty sounds! 'No differentiation' necessary in such opposite rôles as those of Manoah and Harapha; in 'Rejoice greatly' and 'I know that my Redeemer liveth'! Could 'harmonious tone and musical plastics' have enabled Jenny Lind (whose voice was not of the finest character by nature) and Sims Reeves to seize upon the inner meaning of those great Handelian works, and to present them as living entities? The vocalists who have added to mere popularity the power of impressing the thoughtful inner circle have ever been those whose voices reflected thought.

Well does the present writer remember the manner in which a great tenor (Sims Reeves) discussed the mode of expression which he imagined that a leader of God's host would adopt when calling the people to arms. 'He would not,' said he, 'use this kind of voice or tone' (imitating the harmonious yet cramped and untrue 'white' tone of singers of another school). 'He would sing "Sound an alarm" thus,' and lo! by a change of mental and physical attitude he made it clear that he pictured himself as a leader of God's host, the consequence being that his 'Sound an alarm' had a good deal of differentiated emotion in it, not operatic nor bizarre, but noble and suited to the scene. Nor did he seem to trouble himself about 'harmoniousness of tone and musical plastics,' though both were present as the result of spiritual power and fine schooling. He wanted to say, as a man and a musician would say, 'Sound an alarm,' and he said it. This little scene is instructive, for if Sims Reeves was anything, he was a Handelian singer, even as Handel was a master of *bel-canto*; and if Handel's music was anything, it was and is a study in the musical differentiation of emotions. Even Wagner, musician and eloquent actor though he was, never penned a more logical and truthful phrase than the one Handel uses as the musical equivalent to the words 'Thy rebuke hath broken his heart.' The mere fact that this part of the *Messiah* is narrative, does not weaken the argument; on the contrary; it strengthens it. For the subtle judgment necessary to convey the sympathy in the narrator without becoming unduly personal made the task the more difficult. It was an exercise of differentiated human emotion in the contemplation of divine suffering.

The student may safely conclude then that *bel-canto* meant *mastery over the voice*. The legacy it left to mankind was the group of principles for vocal culture with which we are familiar. But this mastery over voice was designed to be a means and not an end. No achievement is ever lost it is, on the contrary, a vantage ground for greater triumph.

Fortunately the tendency of composers is to make vocal music more and more truly histrionic, so that it shall correspond more and more with the inflexions of language. The burden laid upon the vocalists of the future is, therefore, so to carry out the directions of *bel-canto* that nothing written by the composer (provided it be in any sense true to the thought which is in the words) shall be considered impossible by the singer. In all human work there will be limitations, but all musical intervals of any kind whatsoever which are rational and colloquially possible to the cultured man, and are therefore admissible and musically legitimate, shall be considered to be within the range of vocal possibility. On the other hand, refer composers to vocalists as to what they may consider vocal, and you fetter the composer's genius.

This then is the new country which was opened up by the branch line of *bel-canto*. Whatever a musician can write, a singer can—nay, he must—sing. The tyranny of the 'harmonious-sound' has, by musician and singer, been too long allowed to interfere with mental growth and freedom of treatment.

Musical beauty and ideality of voice reside *not* primarily in the sensuous beauty of line and colour, but in the power of developing an absolutely just correlation between the voice and the quick vision of the spiritual man. When that correlation is established, the voice proclaims what the soul sees, and intrinsic ideal beauty is the result.

Spiritual activities are not to be discouraged if art is to grow in power. To tell us that we rant if we talk of genius, and to focus our attention on technique as our *summum bonum*, is to fetter us. Technique and science are indispensable, but a noble creative power compels a noble technique and uses it to express original and unconventional thought. This technical science is shown in musical and poetic vitality, wide as the universe and dependent upon Eternal Spirit. All those whose vocal work is worthy of association with great compositions practically take a leaf out of the composers' book and rear their vocal art-fabric upon the same foundation as musical creators use for theirs. It matters not how the artist may comport himself, he can at the last do no more than present the original composition to his audience. To put it simply, the vocalist does his work worthily when he makes the thought and the sung-word correspond; just as the composer may be said to rise to the situation when he makes the thought in the word and the musical interval and phrase agree with each other.

Very simple and natural, all this; very effective, too. For the supreme powers of the vocal stage have been, not plastic gymnasts or enervating colourists, but men and women who have conveyed through their tone-quality a true and sincere representation of the poet's thought, wedded to the musician's idea of that thought. Line and colour are inseparable from an artist's presentation of the eternal thought or concept, the amalgam of words and music, but they are not the primary force. A poet 'sees down into the heart of things,' a true musician *hears* down into the heart of them. Both poet and musician see and hear with their own eyes and ears, and they reproduce that which they see and hear. The vocalist having disciplined his mind to grasp and his voice to utter poetic-minded thought, listens for the original song, hears it, and says—in effect—'This is how it sounds to me.'

Many internal and external causes have dwarfed our vocal art, but none greater than the suggestion that *bel cantists* were originally musical mountebanks, and that modern vocalists are to be nothing but emotional gymnasts! Created musical thought exists and is the united resultant of music and poetry, being just as surely a structure, for all its invisibility, as that of the architect. The end of all emotional exercise is co-ordinate thought, which is capable of bringing other thought—not necessarily of the same order—into existence; and this thought is manifested in all art-products, musical, pictorial or plastic. The real operatic composer is the man who sets character in the making on the stage; the real singer is the man who reveals character in the act of dealing with thought. To hold the opposite view is to confess oneself the half-grown puppet of a stunted aestheticism. The creative artist passes through emotion to contemplation or sympathetic observation; he leaves mental agitation behind and presses forward to the constructive activity that lies beyond. In the words of Browning ('Pippa Passes'):

> *Shall to produce form out of unshaped stuff*
> *Be Art, and further, to evoke a soul*
> *From form be nothing?*

Character engaged upon characterization is ever more fruitful than emotionalism engaged upon emotion. The stunted aesthete may shriek at those who refuse line and colour as the sole essentials of art, but the full-grown, able-bodied, able-souled artist has no ears for him. Aestheticism lends itself to posing, and the *poseur*-eye sees nothing but posing all around. If we are ever to have natural art we cannot afford to leave out of our reckoning any principle which is characteristic of universal nature. Every mental and psychic quality known to and recognized by sane men must be in 'natural' art. Construction is as characteristic of men as of beavers, which take all they want to construct their dams. The contemplative and the constructive are the goal of the vocal artist.

Differentiation of emotions is then a means to this end, the end being mood-delineation and characterization. These in turn enable the artist to arrive at objective portrayal of character throughout a series of moods and scenes which finally assume proportions of equal magnitude and importance with the composer's work. In a word, emotional activity is the blending of the colours, while singing is the picture painted and finished. At bottom all this amounts to a plea for unity of design. Life is in itself an art-picture in the highest sense, here gloomy, there joyous; and it is the contrast of these elements, and the strength born of their clashings (evidence of mental and psychic growth), which give it value. 'Aestheticism' never yet taught anyone what to do with disenchantment and with agony; but art has so taught men.

To be universal art must take all vital elements into account; must climb every height and sound every depth. The senses and understanding lead us part of the way, the heart and aesthetic intellect help us; but if we would reproduce the conditions which resulted in the greatest works throughout the ages, we must call to our aid the imaginative reason. The wider the outlook, the richer the art. To express co-ordinately the spiritual, moral, intellectual and physical attributes of man is the serious student's aim.

Now these great seers appear always as interested expounders of what they beheld. Performers who re-expound their dream live as interested spectators of the scene, and in all characterization will be the character portrayed—for the time. Nevertheless, the protest of men like M. Coquelin against undue subjugation of the per-former's personality by the rôle he undertakes is pertinent and valuable. This great actor has seen the complete over-mastering of 'self' by the 'counterfeit'; so much tearing of passion to tatters. But while simulation gives a sense of insincere dissimulation, identification results in veri-similitude.

Those who have *lived* their parts have done so by using the whole man, the imaginative reason, the understanding and the senses, to dominate the situation. They have given free play to their capacity for dreaming, for virtual identification with all sorts and conditions of men and characters. They have cultivated moods of abstraction into the conditions of spiritual beings; they have, be it said with deep reverence, felt a certain identification with the Spirit of the Great First Cause. All such consideration results in lofty, imaginative sympathy with great charac-ters, which are manifestations of the might of Eternal Character. Such artists become free and unhampered and enjoy unconscious freedom of spirit. Their body is also free—*anima libera in corpore libero*. The spirit being free to go where it will must realize powerfully all it sees.

The reader has observed that our search for an answer to the question, 'What is singing?' has brought us into touch with various views of technical and spiritual activi-ties. Slowly the belief has grown that the singer's art must embrace the whole of man's nature, and that to be justly called natural this art must deal with all subject-matter known to the mind and soul, as well as to the senses of man. The creative vocal artist will see, hear, feel, imagine all there is to be seen, heard, felt, imagined; he will by force of reason weld the whole into a drama of the invisible—to speak more exactly, into a vocal phenomenon which is inaudible until he calls it forth by weaving its component parts together.

# II

## WHAT IS SINGING?
(*continued*)

WE PUT A QUESTION—'What is singing?'—as do all students. Every singer is practically a definition-seeker. Our question is not easily answered; it calls for serious thought.

As we look round for aid our glance falls upon the composer, who strangely enough seems quite a likely person to help us to an answer—and consequently to a definition. We therefore approach the composer rather than the voice-producer. It takes a rebel to say it, but nevertheless it must be said that voice-production never was the outcome of any special revelation. It should therefore never have challenged the musical and literary intelligence of good composers; this it did when it first said to them, in effect: 'It is impossible for *you* to know how *tone* is made; *tone* is secured in a very peculiar way, and this peculiarity is a *mystery*. The voice-producer is the high-priest of this mystery. You, being only composers, and not voice-producers, are not qualified to speak authoritatively on the subject.' To this the present writer —being also a voice-trainer—ventures to reply that the good composer, as such, is of all people the best qualified to teach *tone* or voice-production; further, that the tone which does not satisfy the composer's brain is wrong. Nor is there anything very alarming in this thought to those of us who are voice-producers, for good composers are ever enthusiastic and generous, ever ready to help the voice-producer in his arduous task. *The singer is no hypnotist, nor is sensuous emotion the end of art.* Such knowledge as the writer possesses of singing, ancient and modern, coupled with his own experience as a singer, will help to answer the question he has been rash enough to raise, namely, 'What is singing?'

Anyone wishing for a practical demonstration—a handy definition, so to speak—will depend on three principles to help him at the start; and indeed ever after.

Firstly, he must breathe deeply; and when we speak of breathing we must include both inspiration and expiration. Secondly, he must be able to sing softly; not that the singer, by means of volition, *makes* a soft tone. If he breathe and sing rightly, the tone will be soft; it cannot be loud at first. An inseparable condition of soft singing is the absolutely unrigid activity of the muscles of the upper part of the body, from the diaphragm upward. By this it is meant that the student is not uncomfortably conscious of the upper part of the body, is not hampered in his articulation. In other words, and thirdly, relaxation is present; not flaccidity; relaxation is the result of consciousness of conserved energy.

These three ideas form the basis of a singer's technique:

(*a*) Breath (deeply taken and deeply controlled).
(*b*) Soft vocalizing (by which is meant soft flow of voice).
(*c*) Relaxation (so that there is no stiffness in the muscles of the chest).

Strictly, (c) is preparatory to (a) and (b).

Having exercised himself thus, when he starts in search of his voice the student will encounter some trouble in securing such a control of his resources as will enable him to produce a voice of adequate resonance. A very vital danger confronts him at this stage, the danger of securing resonance rapidly at all costs. For this resonance is often procured by an unnatural and distorted raising of the palate and forcible downward pressure of the root of the tongue. All such fictitious and forced methods of securing ready-made vocal vesture cannot be too strongly condemned. The texture of the voice must be slowly woven in the loom of time. It is wise to look upon the voice as an instrument, wiser to spend years in perfecting it technically, wisest to add to this the discipline of soul and intellect, that the song which flows through that instrument shall possess all the qualities which go to make a great personality. Thus pursued, technique or mastery over the voice will prove to be an intellectual and a spiritual discipline.

The student, we will further assume, is dissatisfied with mere prettiness of voice, feeling that voice must mean what he wants it to mean, or nothing. It must say, and say artistically, what he wishes it to say. The lyric of a bashful violet or a sunset glow in June may not satisfy the child of mountains and sharp crags. Or fired perchance by some preacher or prophet, nurtured, it may be, amid musical surroundings of an honest and a simple yet lofty sort, such a student might have something original to say; and it is reasonable that he should decide to labour and to incorporate all he has learnt of such natural characteristic in his art.

Any student in such a case would commit a vast error if he began to doubt whether he had the right to express his own thoughts in the manner characteristic of himself. It would be the old story of the fight for survival. The world around has its own thoughts and he has his. He will find that most of his thoughts, those that are of any moment, have occupied a good many poets and musicians before they began to trouble him. As to the way in which he wants to say or sing a thing, he will be wise to make quite sure beforehand that he wants to say or sing it in that particular way. As he grows—if he grows—he will find that his first way is usually modified somewhat. It is nevertheless the same in one respect, namely, that it is his own.

There are, in short, those who feel that they are something more than pretty singers of lyrics. (So many voices are apparently tenorlets of great jugular and cartilaginous purity and limited to about an octave in range.) To all it may be said: 'Cultivate your dramatic gifts; but do not forget that lyric singing is not only a safeguard against the ruin which easily overtakes so-called dramatic singing, but in itself the end of all things in the vocal art. True lyric singing is the most difficult and the most perfect of all singing. But 'pretty' lyric singing becomes truthful lyric singing only when the student has included all kinds of compositions in his vocal repertoire. In a word, lyric and dramatic singing are both indispensable to the vocal student, and each is the complement of the other.'

The student who is true to himself in the best sense will discover that he can get the forces of his soul and body to bear upon his vocal cords. Gradually there will come a ring of truth and sincerity into the singing voice, though that voice may not be large or loud at first, or for some years, it may be. Singing below rather than above his strength, seeking control of line, of time and tune, he will not despise the day of little things. Some original germs communicated to him by his ancestors, and nourished perchance by his own efforts and by his surroundings, are there waiting to come to birth. Nature secretes, and waits till the hour arrives, and then brings out from her store things new and old. She starts from small beginnings; the student of voice must do the same, carrying small, then larger burdens, and training his carrying power to bear the great by first bearing the small.

Too many of us modern singers start with the rôle of Hercules. We dislike the idea of slow growth and hasten to appear in heavy and exacting rôles, whether we are ready or not. True, competition is fierce and opportunities for distinction are scarce; nevertheless, premature decay and ruin are the certain results of an unduly rapid advance. No sculptor starts with statue-making; he first of all learns to model in clay.

Most people, whether they know it or not, are endowed by nature with certain dramatic and musical tendencies, which are there for a purpose and often settle the matter by forcing their way out. Does nature supply us with tendencies without giving us a medium for expressing them, a voice *adequate for the task*? Some such faith is necessary, for the voice and the command over it are for years utterly inadequate to enable many of us to say what we desire to say in our own style. Some years ago a new singer appeared as the Herald in *Lohengrin*. He had been assured that, while he was in himself dramatic, his voice was lyric, and he was warned that to attempt such a rôle meant vocal ruin and professional extinction. It was a trying moment to the young singer; but the inner self triumphed over fear: the attempt was made and proved to be the foundation of his subsequent career. No one is endowed with compelling dramatic instincts and then left without a voice to express them. Nature is too good a workman to make a man dramatic and his voice lyric. If the dramatic is suffered to make its presence felt, it will produce a voice, or it will discover it; for the fact is that the voice is there, whether you use it or not. The voice for you, *your* voice is there. A dramatic man with a lyric voice is an impossibility. Dramatic 'colour' is a mental quality which man imparts to the voice, and is the result of a mental state. The quantity of tone will be affected doubtless by bodily limitations, to a degree; but the quality or the timbre will depend entirely upon the quality of the brain and upon the amount of technique acquired to transmit, through the voice, the dramatic picture conjured up in the singer's brain.

The dramatic is not flesh; it is spirit. The spirit has, of course, to be manifested by the flesh.

To return to the singer who made his first appearance as the Herald in *Lohengrin*, he apparently was somewhat of a rebel. For the benefit of other rebels let it be noted that, unless your cause be right and your preparations adequate, rebellion is dangerous; for the vital principle is that life must be safeguarded and unnecessary exposure and risk avoided. Rebellion has very often proved dangerous, and would have been fatal to the singer whose case we are considering had he not alternately hoped and despaired of his voice for three whole years before the opportunity came of taking the field. He had clung to first principles; had practised his exercises (very simple ones) with his brain. All loud sounds were left severely alone. He never sang anything which might tempt him to launch out vocally; and he gave his throat the opportunity to forget former contortions, thus depriving it of its alleged right to make noises in its own little way. Throats become fixed and habituated to certain positions, in speaking as well as singing. Very few people speak correctly, and consequently when they sing they do not sing correctly. Those, therefore, who have sung as amateurs must become proficient in forgetting former methods and habits.

As a rule, singers at the start sing pieces they ought not to attempt until the primary student-period is over. They will not sing softly, wisely or well; they insist on getting from the very first something which they call tone. What they will, that they sing; and what they will is mostly what the public demands. The public asks more than the singer can safely give before he has rid himself of disabilities which the artificial life of civilization entails upon us. The singer should be cautious and judicious if he desires not to add to the instances of immature and hopelessly distorted use of voice which may be heard from week to week. Vocal decay proceeds with great rapidity and there ensues finally in, alas, too many cases nothing but the hollow clang of a worn-out organ, long before singers have attained to anything like mature intellectual growth. The unconscious pathos of the vocal stage is terrific.

One thing alone justifies the spirit of daring and rebellion and that is faith born of work, wisdom begotten of technique; and the technique must be of the right kind. Empty compliments are fatal, and since vocal inefficiency and decay are prevalent, though it is unpleasant to be compelled to make such pointed allusions to them, they can be cured only if we confess that they exist. Sickness of any sort, undefined and unacknowledged, is full of unpleasant possibilities.

Instrumentalists teach vocalists a valuable lesson in

regard to the importance of technique, shutting themselves up for years in order that they may overcome technical difficulties with assurance. Point after point is assailed with pertinacity. Great pianists practise so as to play technically well; but this is not all, their aim is so to exercise their fingers that they become connecting links between their souls and the keyboard. In other words, their art becomes unconscious. Vocalists can get no better lesson than to listen attentively to great pianists, and especially to violinists, who teach in a pre-eminent manner what melody is. A great violinist is a great singer. Every earnest student recognizes that his work must be centrifugal, that is, the radiating of influences from within outward, and not vice versa. There is assuredly such a thing as a muscular effort, but the happiest results are obtained when the body is disciplined daily to own the sway of the mind; mind *plus* muscle is better than muscle *minus* mind.

Before passing on to purely muscular and technical matters it may be useful to refer to the question of *effort* in singing. Does singing imply effort? *Ars celare artem* is the accepted rule; the effort must not be apparent except for a purpose. A palpable effort, which the vocalist is forced to show, ruins his performance. Reverting to the description of singing as a natural function (in a derivative sense), it would be correct to say that the natural is not effortless. The natural is the result of normal effort; it is undue effort which is unnatural. That effort which goes beyond individual power, and does not utilize all available resources, is not natural. All vital principles must be equally prominent.

Let us proceed to announce baldly in this connection an astounding discovery! The human frame has a lower as well as an upper part, *a back* as well as a front, a fine sounding-board in the roof of the mouth and brilliant resonators in the buccal and nasal cavities; and strangely enough, all these parts are meant to be used in singing! Now, singing which is natural and seems effortless brings all the natural organism into play. Tone is natural and convincing when the whole man is in it. Singing is neither natural nor convincing when there is apparently only a throat, a chest or a diaphragm, an upper without a lower part of the frame to it.

Again, that kind of singing is not natural which displays sensuousness to the omission of intellect, and sacrifices linguistic purity to so-called 'beauty' of tone. A psalm of David calls upon fires and flames, frosts and snows. To chant a universal *Te Deum*, the universe, animate and inanimate, is summoned. The whole spiritual system, spirit, mind, sense and soul, together with the whole muscular system from feet to head, will be in the wise man's singing, and the whole man will be in the tone.

# III

## WHAT IS SINGING?
## (concluded)

THE SENSE OF HEARING is derived from the sense of touch, being an amplification of a function which we may describe as physical. Tone is often called 'touching,' which it is in a physical as well as in a sentimental sense. It is generally imagined that, when one speaks or sings, a something which we call voice or sound issues from the lips and communicates with the drum of the listener's ear. The truth is that nothing in the way of sound proceeds out of the lips at all. Sound has no separate existence; the speaker or singer merely sets air-waves in motion which strike on the drum of the listener's ear, and he—the speaker or singer—thereby communicates with the hearer's brain, wherein results what we call sound. It is no wonder therefore that musicians fall out over tone-quality, when each one hears a different kind of tone! The 'timbre' may be right for one and wrong for another. Composers, too, sometimes disagree over each other's compositions. For it takes two at least to make a 'composition' (as it does to make a tone) for the man who listens.

Hence from the point of view of physics it is more exact

to speak of the human voice as a medium of touch than of sound, the difference being that we use the intervening air as a means of contact. And as the touch of the human hand has its characteristics, so also has the touch of the human voice. There are local, superficial, limp, as well as constitutional, profound, firm touches of the hand, according as the movement culminating in the touch is profound, constitutional, firm, or the reverse. By fixing our attention on the upper part of the body the foundation of our vocal touch is laid too high; too much air being forced to reverberate in the bony and cartilaginous cavities of head and chest, the vocal touch is correspondingly bony and cartilaginous. It is by the co-ordinate activity of the fleshy and muscular parts of the body that both the touch and the voice receive warmth of feeling and become human and artistic. The touch of the superficial breather is hard and inelastic; it has too much of the skeleton in it. Dr. Hans Richter once begged his violinists to 'play with the *meat* of the fingers.' The singer or speaker must employ the *meat*, if his touch (his voice) is to be efficient. As with the physical, so with spiritual qualities —all psychic attributes must contribute their quota. The whole body and the soul must be combined, that the singer may reach the whole of the listener's personality. When this marvel happens, all men must listen. The unity is irresistible. *Omnis porro pulchritudinis forma, unitas est,* said St. Augustine.

If one may use the simile, the chemical fusion of all necessary component elements alone can produce that substance, Voice, which can and does, in a comparative degree at any rate, annihilate space. All legitimate means then must be used—and all natural means are such—for the production of the required results. The required result, in our case, is the product of two forces, inspiratory and expiratory, disciplined into a state of balanced activity acting on the vocal cords and resulting in a controlled expression.

What then are the physical means designed for voice production? They are two:

1. Vocal cords.
2. Breath.

We all know there are two small bands stretched across the larynx which are set in motion by the breath, and so produce 'voice.' A number of organs and muscles affect the action of the vocal cords and of the breath; the management of these various organs and muscles constitutes in one sense the singer's technique. It would be of but small advantage here to reproduce encyclopaedic knowledge in regard to either phonetics or anatomy; it behoves us rather to keep to practical culture and common-sense. Furthermore, neither in speech nor in song can the muscular action of organs be seen, and if they could, there would be but few interesting phenomena to note, while false conditions of breathing make ordinary vocal efforts valueless for purposes of demonstration. We do not therefore propose to reproduce studies in physics. We must be guided by an artistic standard rather than by diagrams of muscles. Our only test will be—artistic results.

Let us first take the vocal cords.

The first requisite for the natural play of these small bands is large liberty. They must be free to do unimpeded work, not pushed and hustled from below, which means fettering their free action; and by the word liberty one indicates the mean between captivity and licence. Captivity of the vocal cords spells 'vibrato,' and licence spells 'wobble.' Nay, the student need not fix his affrighted thought upon his vocal cords, nor regard them as the centre of his existence; the fulcrum of power is not there; no one need fear his vocal cords. They are harmless and inoffensive little things; yet for all that some of us treat them with a good deal of unnecessary severity, the result being that they give forth sounds which do not belong to them, and of which, if the truth were told, they may be heartily ashamed; well treated—they sing.

The mental state (since we must always begin there) which ensures fair and just treatment of the vocal cords is a state of normal relaxation. Take, for example, the state when the blood is vitalized with fresh ozone, when life smiles and all goes well. Now stand before a mirror, glance at the eye, forehead, cheeks, jaw and the general set of the face. To sing in that state would reflect freedom and disembarrassment; the vocal cords would emit truthful singing tones. Just treatment of vocal cords ensures the 'just expression' of which the French speak. Now come, sing to us!

What has happened? Forehead wrinkled, eyes glaring, cheeks hard, jaw set, neck-tendons standing out like whip-cords; and all because we have tried to sing 'Ah' or 'Eh!' But if we were to *say*, merely to pronounce, 'Ah' under the same mental and bodily conditions, with the throat fixed in the same position, it would sound like the 'Ah' of a hobgoblin to frighten children. The farther we go from the heart of Nature the farther we go from just and simple expression; interfere with freedom of movement and we clog the power of utterance. It is useless and worse to disregard this simple fact, simple but very significant: that if we think something worth the thinking (and think it with concentration); say something worth the saying (and say it vividly); do something worth the doing (and do it as if our mind were in it)—we will finally think, say, and do it worthily. Learn separately 'how' to do a thing, that is without reference to the particular 'what' we want to do, and our 'what' will always puzzle us in the doing of it. Forgetfulness of this truth makes students' initial study dull and unedifying and their efforts painful. There is no concentrated mental activity in either, and consequently there is undue physical exertion.

Relaxation is dependent purely on mind, and we have seen that without relaxation the vocal cords cannot work properly. The tone which issues being not a success at first, the student forthwith tries to force the vocal cords to do his bidding. Now forcing is a mistaken policy with willing agents. The student insists upon the vocal cords saying 'Ah,' and that 'Ah' must have what he calls *big tone* in it. Coaxing is better; if they do not obey at once there is a reason for their refusal. The reason why there comes no easy flowing sound from the vocal cords is the fact that they are so *held* that they cannot make such a sound as we want without our hearing the creaking of the machinery; and, further, it is the fact that, without the control of the breath which a co-ordinate muscular activity alone can give, there cannot come at first the loud clear tones so earnestly desired. Without this control the only thing the vocal cords will do, when we set our teeth and say to them, 'You *shall* make a loud tone,' is to make an explosive, blatant, insignificant common-place *noise*.

Now reverse this process. Think easy thoughts; concentrate our mind on sunshine and true sweet sounds, and incorporate them in our 'Ah'; think, look, breathe relaxation, and vocal cords will sigh relaxation contentedly enough. This free unrigid tone, this tone of relaxation, is the basis of all vocal thought. To be sure, the tone will not be such as would make a judicious friend start if he happened to be in the room; he would merely look round and, feeling relaxation, thank us for a pleasant experience. Nor will the phrase or even the note be very prolonged. A long, loud note or phrase is merely a matter of breath control.

The point, however, to observe is that the sound, whether it be a mere whisper or a sung tone, will contain an element of oneself at one's best; of our mind concentrated on a worthy object—an undistorted, unstrangulated self, easy and natural. On such a sound as we have indicated, one can paint or make a real crescendo—a very rare achievement. This kind of tone will take on any colour one can imagine; it will manifest love, hate, pity or fear. It will, it is true, be an infant sound, but it will have life and health in it, and it will grow into manhood broad and deep.

It was once said that the three requisites of a singer are, 1—voice, 2—voice, 3—voice. As well tell a painter that his chief matters are, 1—paint, 2—paint, 3—paint. Of course, a singer must have a voice as a painter must have paints; but the great need of artists is art. Voice is effective—for effect and for money-making; but surely these two are not our chief good. We live for something which cannot be attained by mere voice or money. The future is great in possibilities, which will become actualities for those who choose to make them such.

As with the vocal cords, so with other parts of the vocal mechanism. You, the student, are not to hold your lips thus and so; nor to get your tone forward on to them, nor on to your teeth; nor are you to pin your tongue to any particular part of your mouth; nor to open your mouth in any set mode, nor to brace your shoulders, nor to heave your chest, nor to force open your throat. *All you have to do is to relax and banish fear, and this you do by putting something in its place; you occupy the ground with other thoughts which are to be found in the text and in the music.*

The elemental singing instinct which men have in common with the birds is, without a doubt, at the root of the vocal art. Nor must the instinctive desire for song ever be lost sight of, for out of it comes the power which makes for beauty and charm of voice. But as art grows, so instinct—as the ruling force—must give way to principle. Instinctive, impulsive actions are of comparatively very small importance in the moral world when set side by side with moral actions which have their spring in principle. So in art. Instinct which has developed into principle (without loss of instinct's essentials, be it said) is a far greater power than undeveloped instinct. Through this development a new form of beauty appears. In technique instinct will play a by no means unimportant part. As the student practises, this very force under the direction of reason and imagination will enable him to acquire living, transfusing craftsmanship. The coldly intellectual or the coldly mechanical act is not a human or a natural act. Why then insist for years on superinducing an unnatural and perfunctory state of mind upon the student by making of technique a mere muscular exercise? Why such vocal violence and insincere pretence? and why are linguistic and rhetorical truth almost generally sacrificed to so-called melodic effectiveness? Assuredly it is *technique minus mind* which supplies the reason for this aberration.

The fact is that no one can pronounce 'Ah' without thinking 'Ah.' The 'Ah' must come forth out of an emotional thought. Some situation must be presented to the mind which will call forth 'Ah' in response. So also with all cardinal sounds. The intellect and the imagination must be in active play, and the power of clear thought must be felt at the centre of activity, the mind. This mental activity affects all the organs concerned in technique. When the writer in early days concentrated his attention upon his tongue, he found that this member became stiff and unruly. When, on the other hand, he relaxed mentally, and thought only of what he had to pronounce (the breath being rightly controlled), his tongue reposed peacefully enough in its place at the bottom of his mouth. That is all any well-behaved tongue need do. A great deal of attention is given to this member in many quarters, with the result that the tongue becomes something like a ball in the mouth. Force the tongue, by trying to keep it flat at the bottom of the mouth, and you cannot but vitiate the quality of the tone, making it distorted and unnatural, while pronunciation becomes a thing of the past (or future)!

At the same time leave the larynx as a whole in a state of quiet repose, and the tone and word assume at once a histrionic, eloquent character, whence *l'expression juste*, in embryo, becomes an essential quality without further delay in one's singing. An unrigid larynx means a ruly tongue, and a ruly tongue means simple natural pronunciation. The very singing of 'Ah,' 'Eh,' etc., provided we think them before uttering them, will tilt the tongue so as to differentiate sounds. *All pronouncing which cramps the throat is wrong. There is no part of the vocal range where trickery (so-called vocalizing) is necessary*; no altering of the character of the word is admissible; else you might as well sing in Choctaw and expect people to get the full effect of

English. The so-called 'vocalizing' of a word is a false and lazy procedure. Alter the form and character of the words, and you ruin words and music. The natural principle is: Relax throughout the upper part of the body, relax at the throat, place the burden of tone production on that part of the body which is best able to bear it, namely, the lower, and you will pronounce like a reasonable and an educated being.

We are thus slowly and unconsciously drawing near our consideration of breathing and tone. Having discussed vocal cords and tongue, etc., and the kind of technique which the student will cultivate, we might perhaps remind ourselves that it is ours, as vocal students, to emancipate the tongue, the cavities and the vocal cords, and to offer them no further violence. They are willing servants, obedient to every call, ready to produce the exact resonance, colour and quality which are vocal evidence of thought necessary for characterization and emotional differentiation. They will convey every word and sentiment, actual and ideal, native to humanity. The best way to exercise them is to take a phrase out of a lyric, or out of an aria (*cantilena*), and to treat it as an exercise. Study the context and spend one year—if need be—on the first word; use only deeply controlled breathing, and be not satisfied except when the sung sound is expressive in a simple eloquent manner. All heavy vocal exercises should be avoided at first. Above all, *never vocalize—always sing*.

# IV

## BREATHING

THE SHEET-ANCHOR OF VOCALISTS ought to be pure pronunciation—pure in regard to linguistic fitness and
arising from general culture. Pure pronunciation (musical,
sustained, fitting), once achieved, ensures right tone production, and consequently right tone. Tone which is
correlative to the thought in the word cannot be wrong.
If the character of the tone fit the character of the word,
the tone is essentially just. Every word projects its own
atmosphere, and that atmosphere will be reproduced in
the singer's tone. Singing-tone is true and just when it is
histrionic (as Sarah Bernhardt's or Eleanora Duse's tone
was histrionic). There is perfect correlation between the
tone and the thought which is in the brain and finds
utterance. As good actors' tone fits the word, so also must
good singers' tone fit the word. The sung word should
have the penetrating power which belongs to the fine
elocutionist, whose utterance as such approaches ordinary
speech more nearly than does the singer's, and is also in
general more rationally effective. But ordinary conversational tone could never become a singing tone; and yet it
is a fact that if you change, to an infinitesimal degree, the
character of the word when you sing, making it other than
it is when correctly spoken, your tone *cannot* be the true

tone. If we took the trouble to talk correctly the case might be different.

What are the means whereby we can not only bring the singer's work to the level of the actor's, but even improve upon it? How can we secure the fine pronunciation, the pure linguistic elocution, without which singing is comparatively an imperfect and an insignificant art? As in the treatment of vocal cords all physiological terms were studiously avoided, so also in regard to breathing we keep as clear as we can of the shibboleths of the schools. Every person who chooses to be docile can apply the following simple principle: Breathe with the lower rather than with the upper part of the trunk; he who breathes with the upper and forgets that he has a lower part to his trunk is sure to fail as a singer.

The writer during his early training made this error and felt famished for air when engaged at his studies in singing. We have the lower as well as the upper part of the body to deal with. In truth, it is the lower rather than the upper part that is our concern. There *is* a lower part to the trunk. Our learned friend smiles, but so many people forget the fact! We are conscious of the upper part during respiration, and so much bother is made about the singer's chest that it astonished the writer when he discovered that his strength lay in the lower part, and, as has been said, when he found that he had a back and that the trunk was poised on two good pedestals. Strangest of all was it to find that it was possible to bring every energetic force in the body and its supports to bear upon the diaphragm, *directly or indirectly*, and consequently upon the vocal cords.

The action of the muscular system as a whole upon the singing organism has never been fully demonstrated. It would certainly seem to be a fact that there is a supplementary and co-ordinate power which can be developed throughout the whole muscular system from the feet upward, the effect of which can be distinctly felt both upon the diaphragm and the vocal cords. Yet no one needs to make war upon his diaphragm or force it in two months to do the work it demands two years to accomplish. All safe athletic training is slow and gentle; so also is artistic training. The diaphragm will work effectively if it be helped by the muscles directly connected with it; these muscles again are helped by their co-ordinate muscles. But if the diaphragm has to carry the whole weight which should be proportionately distributed throughout the body, it will fail and the singer will gasp. Again, if the muscles connected with the diaphragm are bereft of the sympathy of the great muscles of the thighs and the legs, they too lose heart and ocasionally fail us. Distribution or subdivision of labour is essential and natural.

Curiously enough, the vocal cords and the diaphragm are at first sworn foes—to all appearances. Relax at the throat, give the vocal cords their freedom, thus throwing on the diaphragm the task of controlling the breath, and that organ most ungraciously refuses the task. On the other hand, the vocal cords refuse to speak graciously when the diaphragm demands the right. Very difficult the writer found it to promote an agreement between these two seemingly belligerent forces. The reason probably was this—that it is not easy to persuade the human brain to think of two things at once. Long and weary was the continuance of this puzzle to the writer. At last came the key which Nature supplied. Conservation of energy was her solution of the difficulty. 'Get all necessary breath and keep it, without rigidity or undue effort,' such was her counsel. One does not need a Nasmyth hammer to crack a nut, and the nut the singer has to crack at first is a little one. Procure the necessary amount of breath to make a whisper and then convert it into tone. That is all. But see that you waste no breath; sigh contentedly and slowly; then take a breath as deep as that sigh. When you have it, keep it; then sigh it out slowly and under control, so that you could suddenly press more or press less, at will, with the muscles of the abdomen and the back, and could stop the sigh if you desired. There must be no hissing noise. After doing this several times, convert the whisper into tone. Begin to sing *instantly* when you have your singing breath under control; do not wait to think, sing at once and make use of your motive force, or you will waste it. There must be no escape, no waste of breath, no collapse of the diaphragm—even to the extent of a hair's breadth.

The diaphragm will show you at once by its position whether there be any escape of breath, for it will have collapsed; your throat will tell you the same story, for it will be rigid; the quality of your whisper will confirm the evidence, for it will be hissing unnaturally. Sane people do not hiss. Your ear will help you to knowledge. The training of the ear is one-half of the training of the voice, but your mind is the court of appeal when in doubt.

Let us say it all again. Take a little breath, deep as a contented sigh; preserve it at the diaphragm, and be not prodigal at the start; if you are wasting breath, or have taken too little, your face will tell the tale, for it will look anxious, and your eyes will be staring. After a deep, easy inhalation (with no heaving of shoulders or of chest), keep the breath under deep control, and do not imagine you are dividing yourself in two at the point where the diaphragm makes its outer rim apparent. Remember the power your mind has over your muscles and use the whole muscular system co-ordinately—from below upward. Think 'control' (by means of the muscular system) and control will finally come. A good deep breath will manifest itself by a tidal filling up of the trunk with breath, in the anterior, the dorsal and the lateral regions, all round the waist. The body will swell gently (not heave) in front, at the back and at the sides. A good control of breath will make itself apparent by the absence of any sudden collapse at any one of the three (more properly four) points mentioned. Enormously strong muscles are brought into play to help the diaphragm, but no proper use can be made of them if the mind thinks of the breathing function as though it were performed from above-down instead of from below-upward.

Breathe with the will, intelligently, thoughtfully, slowly, and you will have no trouble with the vocal cords; nor will you be vexed by weak spots, breaks, registers or any other of the paraphernalia supplied by credulity to charlatanism, which, greedy of its ease, plays the sphinx and the mountebank at one and the same time. If this sentence seems a trifle severe, the reader must please think of the useless torture to which thousands of students have been subjected through indefinite and insincere 'instructions.' How many a poor pupil has become a practical monomaniac on the subject of 'that break in my voice between D and D sharp.'

A deeply controlled breath ensures free action for the larynx and the pronouncing apparatus. Lack of freedom paralyses art.

Breathing is of two kinds, undisciplined (customary) and disciplined (acquired); the breathing of the general public and that of the professional-breather. The last has been divided into many kinds. The battle of the breathers has raged from continent to continent (some speak of killing with a look; here we kill with a breath!). All combatants are perhaps agreed on one point, that the singer's breath is an acquired one of some kind, and yes, they agree on one more point, namely, that 'orthodoxy's my doxy, heterodoxy's yours.' Experimentalists have from time to time heard famous singers, watched their breathing, and in proportion as the singers produced a '*pleasing*' tone have with due emphasis pronounced for diaphragmatic, thoracic, clavicular or abdominal breathing. It is well to be grateful for small mercies. The world has been slowly gathering knowledge—which, however, may need a little sifting before it can be called wisdom.

Nasal, frontal, jugular, gutteral tones have their adherents; moreover, numberless tendencies (inherited and acquired), predisposing men to be broad or narrow in character, affect their senses, including the sense of hearing, and their critical faculty. There are accordingly many and various opinions as to what kind of tone is right. *Diversos diversa juvant.*

Apparently this diversity of taste in tones must account for the existence of the different schools of breathing. The point of view is everything; according as musicians lean toward decorativeness or verisimilitude, the question of vocal right and wrong and their contributory bodily conditions will be variously decided. Vocal 'power' and 'charm' carry us away. The truth is that few realize the immense hypnotic power of the human voice. Before accusing the writer of wishing to do away with real charm and instinctive beauty of voice, let the good reader suspend judgment. The contention it is desired to make is that to charm and instinct something else must be added, so that we may finally rejoice over a new amalgam.

Such singers as Sims Reeves and Jean de Reszke have not lived in vain. What have they taught us? Refusing to range themselves on the side of any particular school of singing and breathing, they lived their artistic lives not by the senses alone, in spite of the fact that they had vocal idiosyncrasies inseparable from their style and physical constitutions. To Sims Reeves nothing in the way of vocal expression came amiss; he traversed its whole range, from the airiest comedy to the deepest tragedy, with verisimilitude. The lofty-spiritual, the heroic, the tender and emotional, every tone of love, hate, scorn, fear, faith, doubt, prayer, joy, sorrow, came from this singer's soul with authority, conviction and truth. Jean de Reszke has given us like results in Wagner-drama and in opera, his work dealing entirely with romance and mythology. The mastery obtained by these two artists over their voices was of a mental as well as physical character—a fact which affected their breathing.

The tone of voice which most appeals to the dominating principle in men's lives—to the supreme emotion or passion which is their chief characteristic—is the tone which they will pronounce true. Some men are gentle, some forceful, some sensuous, some intellectual; again, one man is of narrow vision, another broadly sympathetic; one small-minded, another generous; one a pretentious *poseur*, another a lover of things as they are, who seeks for bed-rock truth. Diversity of opinion in regard to tone-quality indicates this diversity of character, and this diversity obtains until the man of genius sweeps all away by the whirlwind of his power and wakens the elemental greatness which belongs to humanity in virtue of the rock whence it was hewn. They who study the technique of singing will accept those bodily conditions as correct which produce the tones they most admire; we have, accordingly, many schools of breathing.

The progressive student will adopt only that kind of breathing which gives him universal tone, that is to say, such a tone as will serve for all characterization. One kind of tone, fixed and unchangeable, however sensuously beautiful it may be, will not satisfy him. Experience has taught the world that the really sane man is he whose hereditary and acquired forces, physical and psychical, have worked harmoniously, so as to produce a balance of character and of mind which enable him to make harmonious comments upon the pregnant situations of life. So in art the verdict of experience is in favour of that man who through perfect balance of parts, physical and psychic, produces a harmoniously sane tone with which he can make true musical pronouncements upon any musical and dramatic situation that may present itself to him. A 'beautiful' voice undeniably produces hypnotization, and excites frenzy; but the singer who wants to be a factor in human progress cannot satisfy himself by playing the hypnotist.

Tone is an index to character; the thoughtful singer will therefore set about establishing a high standard for himself and will seek such methods as will enable him to realize that standard. Breathing is an integral part of the true method of tone production; indeed, in one sense the root of the matter. Any kind of breath the weight of which is unduly felt at any given part of the body is apt to produce a tone that betrays the part of the body thus unduly affected. The tone will be inelastic and unfit for instant varied and universal expression. All limitation of the breathing function produces a corresponding degree of limitation and localization of tone. Mental adaptability and physical elasticity underlie universality of tone. The whole subject, however, is so polemical that one is glad to have a definite case of achievement to point to. The two great artists to whom we have alluded accomplished such a result and were not fettered vocally, while their outlook has been large and comprehensive, and their bodily aspects clearly indicative of constitutional, and not of local, breathing. Their faces expressed alert receptivity, expansiveness and relaxation and were not disfigured by any one kind of sentiment, emotion or thought. Meeting either you would say, 'There goes a man and an artist.' Their attitude on the stage was free, easy, and unconstrained. They showed no rigidity, no embarrassment at any point, when they breathed. Jean de Reszke favoured the writer by allowing him to make a rapid study of his breathing while he sang. He did not give the idea of effort; he breathed constitutionally; he was mentally active; his soul was in his work and his soul 'went everywhere.' He sang a patter song of the *café chantant* in answer to a remark that a great artist must sing a comic song as well as music-drama. Everything singable must be sung (not necessarily in public).

Now this kind of singing is impossible if any breath be allowed to escape unconverted into tone. (The old *bel-cantists'* test of good breathing and singing was to hold a lighted taper in front of the lips; if the taper flickered, breathing and singing were pronounced bad.) The face must wear a singing look, and the look must be of the same character as the tone—say the same thing. This can never be if the breathing is rigid, for a rigid posture and breathing conveys only rigidity. From the mind must start the impulse which results in the perfect union of the look on the face, of gesture (in acting) and of the tone of voice—all three making one expression.

The singer's breathing is an act of volition which becomes, finally, an unconscious one. To realize this is to realize the required physical conditions; to breathe deeply and control deeply with the whole body from below upward; then judge of the correctness according as we are able to say, 'I love,' 'I hate,' 'I pray,' 'I believe,' 'I pity,' 'I beseech,' 'I defy,' etc., with, in each case, appropriate tone, and without deliberately altering the pose of the throat or the form and character of the words.

Such is our counsel to the student. He must remember that the body depends on the mind for its inspiration—in both senses. He must breathe easily and generously, and he must say what he finds he wants to say, whether as singer or actor. If he cannot fully express himself as poetic-elocutionist, vocal-painter or musician endowed with the seer's gift, there is something wrong with his breathing. Very probably he is breathing too much. It is not the amount of breath a man takes that tells, but the amount he controls. If, after absorbing the spirit of the text, he finds he cannot reproduce that spirit, let him look to his breathing. There may be different opinions regarding tone-quality; but on the point we have just been discussing there can be but one.

The singer, having acquired a natural system of breathing, in the constitutional sense, will ask himself a few questions: (a) Can I sustain my tone firmly? (b) Can I give full value to vowels? (c) Can I musicalize consonants? (d) Can I pronounce justly and intelligently, as I do when I speak with sustained breath? (e) Can I show clearly whether I am a prophet, a soldier, a lover or a cobbler (who may be all three) when I sing the rôles which deal with these characters severally? If the answer be 'yes,' his breathing is correct. The quality of his tone will depend upon that of his mind—his soul, and not merely upon physical considerations.

Irresistibly we are drawn to the conclusion that right breathing can only be judged by right tone; and that right tone can only be judged by the *summum bonum* of the singer, namely, pronunciation—pure and truthful in every part of the voice, high or low. The word, with its atmosphere, is the test. Pronounce with refinement, with the quick wit of rational and imaginative beings, and your tone will be right. Breathe so that you pronounce rightly, and you breathe rightly. But if you breathe so that you must vocalize—in the narrow and pedantic sense—you breathe wrongly. When you convey the impression that the words you sing are those of the character you represent, when mood and atmosphere are characterful, you must be breathing correctly. Once the truly natural, normal breathing described in this chapter has been acquired, a singer's equipment is merely a matter of brains, sur-roundings and development. 'Ah,' 'Eh,' 'Ih,' etc., *coloratura* and *cantilene* are easily dealt with. Sympathy and the legitimate pressing-out which conveys the human ele-ment to the voice, relieving it of the 'whiteness' which is the bane of modern singing, will reward the patient and intelligent student. (By 'whiteness' of the voice we mean something which, though flexible and brilliant enough, is deficient in real sympathy and expression, and lacking in verisimilitude.)

Singers suffer tortures from nervousness. The best and only cure for this malady is a good deep breath, well and deeply controlled. It enables one to collect one's thoughts;

and the first thing a serious singer does when he has called his thoughts home is to *empty himself of himself, and put the thought of his work in place of the selfish fear that possessed him*. To cure nervousness put something in its place; occupy yourself with the scene you are about to depict and nervousness will flee as mists before the sun. If the attack be a bad one, make a still more determined effort to evict self and secure a new tenant. 'As thy day, so shall thy strength be.'

# V

## TONE

HUMAN TONE *is indissolubly allied to speech. We can make no tone which will not be simultaneously a word or a part of one.* This statement must not be wrested from its context and forced to mean that the making of a musical vocal tone, *ipso facto*, forms intelligible speech. Whatever may be the truth concerning the immediate purpose of the evolution of tone, there can be no doubt, in the light of the design revealed by the ethical process and social life, that its ultimate purpose is the communication of thought. The making of the tone makes the word, or a part of it; but the word, or a part of it, is the immediate cause of making the tone; as the tone was evolved for the sake of the word, the word may therefore be said to be the important factor. A similar argument though not complete in every detail holds good in regard to thoughts and words. We can have no definite thoughts without words, though we can have words without thoughts, and, indeed, frequently do. There must be some medium, and a musician's 'thought' is formulated and conveyed by means of notes. It is thought therefore that takes precedence.

The chain then is: 1, Thought; 2, Word; 3, Tone. Now, 1 (Thought) and 3 (Tone) must be intimately connected—there must be complete fusion—and Tone must reflect Thought or be judged imperfect and insignificant. There would be no such thing as a human tone were it not for the mental and emotional activity. Man being gregarious, tone becomes the medium of intelligent intercommunication, of thought-exchange. But a thought in its purity cannot reveal itself without a pure medium; hence, if the tone is to do its work properly, it must give the whole of the thought which is in the word, with its atmosphere. This it does when it gives *the word as it is*. The mind conceiving that which seeks an outlet in utterance the result is voice, pure and simple—at first, the superficial, clavicular, sternal or laryngeal utterance characteristic of a large portion of humanity. Vocal efficiency depends on mental efficiency; the character of the mind is accordingly of supreme importance to that of tone.

The method which some of us have found useful in converting this superficial utterance into a singing voice has been discussed, the method being compact of mental and physical discipline. Forces are called in for the purpose which are not used in ordinary speech, though a speaking voice properly trained would naturally make a better singing voice than an ordinary speaking voice.

The mind then is the starting-point, holding within it an emotional thought which seeks an outlet. It follows that we must so govern tonal vibrations and inflexion that the thing expressed is the thought in possession of that mind, and nothing else; there must be no foreign matter. Voice, tone, sound exist for this purpose in speech (disciplined or undisciplined) and in song. It is for the singer to discover exactly what disposition of the human frame will enable him to secure such a pronunciation of the word as will make that word the articulate expression of the mental concept it stands for. *The character of the word, accordingly, and not that of the tone—as such—is the safeguard*; and as the word is the thought made audible, it follows that the *mind, not the senses, must be regarded as the voice-trainer*. Ill-educated coarseness can neither teach nor produce tone. Fine mind produces fine pronunciation, and voice must needs follow with discipline and technique. Voice training is complicated by using fanciful 'voice builders'; jargon and gibberish are not 'thoughtful.' Rather let a man project his mind (a very small portion of it at a time) through the medium of the uttered word; let him say what he wants to say musically and poetically, lyrically or dramatically, with linguistic purity, and his voice must be of the fine and right kind.

*A student's aim should be to sing a word, rather than to make a tone.* Fine pronunciation being the result of mental and bodily discipline, fine tone is its inseparable companion. Elocution and tone are simultaneous studies. The writer struggled with the disadvantages of a throaty tenor and a guttural bass, but he never enjoyed the privilege of being taught elocution. He had an ideal (it grew slowly) which came in part from his observation of those who had *thought* themselves into a state of true and just expression. No stilted, labial, dental or laryngeal mannerism can possibly produce anything like the unconscious art which marks the real elocutionist. Under the guidance of mind therefore we study so as to utter justly the thoughts which pass through the mind; and as we study, our power over singing and pronunciation grows. The colour of correctly spoken, and the sustained rhythm of sung, words constitute the whole of the vocal art.

But what constitutes pronunciation? It is not the mere physical act of forming the vowels and consonants that go to make the word; rather let us call it the saying of the unified mental thing which comes into vocal existence when the vowels and consonants—the verbal representatives of that thing—are uttered. The student first thinks the word clearly, and listens to it with his inner ear; when the mind has sounded it, he says it calmly with his voice. This is the finest singing lesson a man can have.

In the case of the great singer we have named, his whole face, his whole being, pronounced the words; he used his imaginative reason; his mind saw all it could see. Fine pronunciation will ever depend on that. The great tenor realized, for example, 'Samson's' (a strong man's) blindness, so that when he reached his climax in the words, 'Sun, moon and stars, all dark to me,' there was a horror of darkness about his pronunciation which lives yet, somewhere, in this most laryngeal world of ours. Here was an example of what a singer can do in the way of projected realism. It is true that Sims Reeves, with his strong physique, his great column of a throat from which he loosely shook his voice, and his massive frame, was specially endowed physically. But it was his mind that made him. Some years ago his first words to the writer, who had sought his aid in regard to the singing of *Elijah*, were, 'What do you think about the prophet—what sort of man was he?' No word of thoracic, crico-thyroidal, or epiglottic matters!

An interesting point for vocalists may be given here, which the same singer communicated. He showed how the control of breath gave the impression of the uninterrupted line, even when the actual tone was discontinued so as to take a comma into consideration. This is a subtle and delicate vocal-principle. The moral of all this is, that the saying of the words with special reference to the character portrayed is essential. The whole man must utter the text, and the mind—the throat obeying the mind's message and contentedly becoming a channel for clear, atmospheric utterance. Students will be careful to make it appear that the characters they portray knew their grammar, prosody and punctuation and were keenly alive to the necessity of preserving their musical and poetic instincts from violation. They must never force the situation, and in that case they will never force their voice.

Characters too must be differentiated. A tenor is in error who converts Obadiah's music in *Elijah* into a conventionally lyrical lovesick methodist wail. No artistically sane baritone bellows 'Was duftet doch der Flieder'; the influence of Hans Sachs's poetry (*Die Meistersinger*) and the soft-falling mantle of night will cause him to sigh out his opening phrases in this great monologue. Tone-production and articulation go hand in hand, for without articulation and its primal cause there would have been no tone. If anyone dissent from this proposition, let him take any word as a test, or any phrase. And first, let us take an easy breath, deep as a sigh of deep content. Control the breath in the same place as it was felt when first sighed and afterward inhaled. Now whisper the word, non-hissingly; then sing (whisper converted into tone); and again whisper non-hissingly. All this on one breath, without hurry, but also without waste of time. If the word sound fairly convincing, the tone, though comparatively subdued, will be fairly correct even in the case of a novice. Let an ordinary student, however, after singing the word, speak it immediately, without taking a fresh breath, leaving the throat as it was while he sang, and he will find how utterly the values are changed. The word will sound quite different to what it would be under right conditions. Most people think they can say or sing 'Ah' so that there is nothing but 'Ah' in it, and that therefore all that 'Ah' implies, when spoken with intention, is in it. But can they? In all the cases which have come under the writer's notice, professionally, the tone is meaningless and white, for it is invariably obtained by sacrificing the essential qualities of the spoken word (spoken, that is to say, under natural and artistic conditions). Let an untrained baritone sing the words, 'As God the Lord of Israel liveth,' etc. (the opening phrase in Mendelssohn's *Elijah*), and then, without taking fresh breath, *say* the words he has just sung, with the same jugular contortion and clavicular upheaval, and he will find some food for reflection. It will prove his articulation to be fictitious and insincere, and his prophet a 'harmonious blacksmith.'

Much has been written concerning man's *two voices*, the singing and the speaking. Man has but one; two he does not need. If truly normal breathing were cultivated, and clear enunciation fostered, there would be less nonsense talked about the divisibility of the voice into two kinds. Further, if the experiment here suggested were made in our schools, if children were taught proper respiration and due control of breath by means of sustained thought, and were moreover trained to secure a focus for thought through its concentration in words (pure thoughts in pure words), our contention could not fail to be generally accepted. Singing and speaking are, of course, different functions; but speaking affects singing, though the two be not synonymous. Speaking, reading and declamation are, however, integral factors of singing, and our contention is that, while we are put off with a sound which is merely *suggestive* of the word in ordinary and even in public speech, we shall never have general efficiency in our public speakers and singers. We understand each other only by the general effect of the sound of the words, and our vocabulary is not a very large one; difficulty of understanding ensues instantly when a rarely used word is employed, and we accordingly find it hard to grasp quickly what the strange word is.

The best and most effective speakers and preachers have always been those who *sustained* their tone (not in sing-song fashion, however). They gave a sustainedly vocal character to their speech, without any droning, but also without jerkily popping out their words like so many corks. The words are floated out on a current of flowing breath. The late Sir John Stainer informed the writer years ago that the late Canon Liddon carried this method to such a pitch that at times he almost gave the impression that he preached on a melody—so keen was his sense of sustaining. Sir John Stainer also frequently took the Canon's note on the organ, quietly, and found that his reciting note would frequently be the high tenor A and that he would sometimes touch the high C, flowingly and sustainedly. It is well remembered that this preacher was most easily audible even in the vast dome of St. Paul's Cathedral. A popular fallacy claims that a manly voice is very deep, loud and guttural. One has heard it on the stage and sometimes in clubs. It may be very useful for ghosts and non-comic grave-diggers; but it is monotonous and hollow, nor can it ever produce the thrill of realism. The deep tone is always sombre and should be used but sparingly. The middle tones (in pitch) form the best starting-point for the public speaker, intensity being easily secured by a slight elevation in the pitch and a slight pressure on the voice. So-called deep reverberatory voices, which advertise their possessors by making loud noises when they are close at hand, never carry in large halls.

Combining what has been said on general inefficiency in speech and the best way to cure it, and on the cause of eminence in public speakers with what has been already set forth in regard to singing and voice-production, we pin our faith to the following principle: *The voice of the future must prove that it grows out of language; and singers must begin their studentship with the singing of thoughts; for thought is the fount of language, and language the fount of tone.*

We may perhaps venture, at this point, to sketch a singer's progress—how he goes from strength to strength:

A poet, for instance, makes his poem.

A musician reads the poem, appreciates its structure and its matter, and makes his comment after his kind on what the poet has seen; he feels the effect the vision had upon the poet in the first instance, and reflects its influence —that of the poetry. The musician builds his structure with notes, which are his words; these he forms into phrases, as the poet with words. There ensues a musician's poem.

A singer in whom song-instinct stirs sees and appreciates the structure of the poet and musician, and reproduces it by means of thought, words and melody before the mind's eye, through the senses. The singer is therefore a reproducer of a twice-erected structure, and this is his song. But no man builds without leaving a part of himself in the building; the musician accordingly adds something to the original poem, and the singer to the original poem and music, although he never alters the form of a word or of a phrase. Nay, that which he adds he does not set out to add—he does it unconsciously. The poet sees and speaks, the composer hears and translates into musical language, while the singer reads and absorbs the original and the translation and reproduces them by means of appropriate voice. All vocal students will therefore see that their pronunciation and thought must be correlative to each other, and to the poet's and musician's.

Elastic, expansive, appropriate, musicalized, sustained *pronouncing* will do more for him and his tone than all the babel of the breathing and voice-producing sects can ever do. Lovely, just, vivid pronunciation will make any method *teres atque rotundus* (smooth and round). In our day the *ore rotundo* (the round mouth) has degenerated into a parallelogram. But pure pronunciation is within our reach; general culture brings it there, in spite of all charlatanism and sphinxdom. He who pronounces with the upper, without regard to the lower part of the trunk, thereby failing to help lips, tongue, cheek and jaw by mentally relating them to the lower part, vitiates his tone. Embarrassment in saying any word, or in changing from one word to another, communicates embarrassment at once to the tone. Any musical person who speaks musically, that is, with rhythmic varied intonation, and has learnt to recite, can learn to sing. The reciter's characteristics will remain in the singer, but to his reciting will be added singing power when he shall have learnt to speak his varied thoughts frankly on a sustained diaphragm or breath. *Power of sustained breath means power of sustained tone, which is nothing in the world but sustained thought made audible.* This is not fancy; it is proved fact, proved moreover by the writer's own experience.

Such, however, is the depth to which hocus-pocus has brought this art of singing that great composers, men of light and leading, feel constrained to tell you frankly, 'Of course I do not know anything about singing.' And yet singing is an important branch of the musical art. Every man who has intellect and emotion added to musical knowledge (and the composer possesses all three) knows and ought to know all about singing, if he uses his powers at all to judge of it. We shall not all suddenly attain the highest results; with special endowments go special results. But every musical human being who can hear and talk can also, with discipline, sing sufficiently well to justify himself in dealing vocally with the songs of Schubert, Franz and the rest. It is astonishing how a voice will grow at both extremities. Disabilities disappear, and new capabilities come to light. The writer's own voice at first contained an octave and a fourth, with always a crack on the highest note. Training has given him just one additional octave.

People who have singing voices are those who have so wished to sing that their desire has overcome the fear of their inability to sing. The voice grows by use. We have never heard of a person starting suddenly to produce great vocal power without previous vocal activity of some kind. Many say they would like to sing 'better than anything on earth'; but the desire is not so overwhelming as to force them to try to sing, and singing means hard work, and 'hard work is such a bore.' The result is that comparative atrophy sets in and a possibly useful singer is lost to the world. Voice too feeds on voice. All Welsh people sing and have singing voices; everyone is born into a singing atmosphere and the desire to sing grows; the soul sings, and the body reflects the song, with varying degrees of efficiency. There will always be grades. But the writer's experience emboldens him to say that all who have ordinary speaking voices, who know their notes and have the sense of pitch and rhythm (both these senses improve with practice), can be taught to sing well, even though they may have considered themselves 'voiceless.'

As a test case the writer took as a pupil a man who had never sung, and thought and said he had no voice, but who was musical and educated. His education had made him plastic, and he had grit and could therefore bring himself to do exactly as he was told. Having been present at a lecture on 'voice,' he came in answer to a statement made during that lecture. After some little discussion a start was made. At first there was nothing but a jugular gurgle; there was *no tone of any sort*. At the second lesson this pupil sang a song by Franz respectably, and in six weeks he could sing, with a fairly crisp and sympathetic voice, arias from *The Creation*, *Messiah*, *Elijah*, etc. He went steadily on, improving in volume of voice (which extended to two octaves in range) and in control over it. His musical recitations, essential to a singer's training, were also quite noteworthy. He was a Harvard graduate, a lawyer of distinction in New York, and was over thirty years of age when he began his vocal studies.

Jean de Reszke once said to the writer, 'One must sing as one talks.' 'Yes,' was the rejoinder, 'and one must talk as one sings'—that is, rightly. Talk on an absolutely balanced breath control; unclasp the fingers of a rigid civilization from off your throat! The whole body, from the heels up, will be in the phrase, if—as there cannot be any grave doubt—the theory of reflex action be true. Singers as a rule avoid much speaking before they sing. In March 1901 the writer made a six hours' continuous use of the 'speaking voice' and one hour's use of the same voice in singing. There was no trace of hoarseness or fatigue in the voice at the end. Any local strain would have made such a performance impossible.

The writer has never known what a clerical sore throat is, and has on different occasions sung when suffering from bronchitis, laryngitis, and the like—without betraying to the public any distress. All this is practical proof of the soundness of the contentions to be found in this volume, and is given purely in their support and merely as a record of fact. A good singer must reflect good tones.

# VI

## TONE
### (concluded)

A CURSORY GLANCE at a theory has before now afforded ground for a disingenuous, incomplete and ridiculous comment. It is therefore perhaps necessary to point out that singing and speaking are *not* synonymous and that we do not hold the mental and physical activities to be identical in the two functions. Further, though it be truly argued that fundamentally the conditions underlying pure speech and song are identical, yet in practice there are certain points of difference between the two, as will presently be seen.

Among some five ways of ordinary vocal communication, namely, in ordinary speech, reading aloud, public speaking, the actor's speech and in singing, the effective use of all five depends fundamentally on the same principles. The difference between the various modes of performance is a difference of subject, purpose and style on which man exercises his practical, spiritual and aesthetic capabilities. In the evolution of language philologists recognize ease-of-pronunciation as a factor in the gradual formation of words. Must we therefore be content when man utters those words with the least possible trouble to himself? We are all a little lazy; so long as the general sense is fairly clear, why trouble about so very 'unimportant' a matter as pure pronunciation? When wrong pronunciation or bad diction come to be regarded as equally reprehensible with a wrong choice of words, we may see this subject ventilated. For while corruption of language is a fully recognized fact, defective utterance (which could be cured) carries it to its extreme limit.

Languages as we find them are the instruments which poets and musicians have used to bring about their creations. Surely it were well for us if we employed the words of genius with appropriate colour and completeness. Language is, moreover, the evolved thought of a nation, and is strongly characteristic of that nation; but really expressive talking is a rarity. Besides, there is such a thing as typical cultured diction. Public improvement in this regard would raise the standard of utterance in Church and State. The language of the collects and of the form of public prayer is noble. We do not hear it in church. When conversational speech is become formful as well as intelligible; homilectic speech simple, true and unaffected; when public reading is appropriate and histrionic speech informed with real-seeming—singing also will have to look to its sovereignty. 'Levelling-up' will raise the standard. But the public has this in its keeping, once its ear has been won.

Why is it that imperfect vocal methods are no bar to popularity? The reply is that anything is good until a better appears. The public ear, unless the true and the false be heard on the same stage at the same performance, does not remember from day to day what a voice is like; at any rate it cannot always analyse its essentials. There may be an idea that a voice was loud, big, pretty, and that it stimulated emotion. Effects are made; the more superficial, the greater the applause and the excitement. Charlatanism and advertisement draw large crowds and large sums for a time. The power that elevates, strengthens, and inspires is of another kind and is not popular. We have not yet reached Utopia, and so the singer must cultivate frugality.

Let it be said again that talking, lecturing, reading aloud, preaching, acting and singing are, as to technique, closely related. The first requires less sustained effort than the others, as is reasonable, seeing that it is a constantly recurring task. Life's ordinary affairs require less sustained mental effort than the affairs of art, and this it is which represents the real difference between talking and lecturing, reading aloud, preaching, etc. In all public efforts the tone (made manifest by vowels and consonants) is more sustained, as is the mental and spiritual effort, there being a larger field of intellectual and spiritual activity to traverse and a larger space to fill. That which must guide the performer in the choice of a suitable manner (whether the task be lecturing, preaching, acting, or singing) is purely aesthetic power; his success will be commensurate with his power of mental transformation.

In the case of the singer some persons demand that the performer must always be 'pleasing' to the senses, whatever the character of the rôle he undertakes. This, in judging vocalization, is an error—a pleasing Mime, for instance, or a Mephistopheles who is an example of light, flippant comedy! (Gounod suffers at the hands of his interpreters.) It is not here suggested that the tone should be made grotesque or ugly—by artifice. All that one would wish would be such a tone as a real Mime would use, the tone of a morally crooked mean dwarf, or that of a Mephistopheles which would convey the hate, the mockery and moral ugliness of the spirit which confounds vice with virtue and rejoices in the task. Again, Beckmesser is often clowned, being represented as a lover of mirth-provoking antics, while Wagner's creation is an acknowledged master-singer—a keen critic according to his lights and a man who was certainly much in earnest. To *clown* the part is a sorry way out of the difficulty of *singing* it with appropriate colour.

To return: reading, preaching, acting and singing depend for their efficient practice on the same vocal principles. Though differing in subject, object and style of treatment, as far as the technical voice is concerned it is, or it ought to be, the same in all, with this difference, that the singing voice is necessarily *more sustained* than the others. For the singer perfection is only reached when tone is ever present; when vowel is merged in vowel, word joined to word without a break; when there is, so to speak, no 'daylight' between one word and another. In such case the musical phrase is preserved as it should be, as an entity, while the value of the poetic phrase is not lost. The singer, having many difficulties to overcome, his struggle with his failures will be lightened by clinging to a few ideals and by reducing every question, as far as he can, to its unit. Let him seek for the foundation of all art and universal principle running through the whole phenomenon. On thus considering his own art he will come to the conclusion that beauty apart from justness is unattainable, tone without mind a vanity, aesthetics without ethics a snare. In this way only may cause and effect be yoked together, and the work will be done for the love of it, material advantage often lying in another direction. It will be the artist's joy even to agonize in order to try and include the human, the divine and art (a manifestation of both) in one great energy.

In this correlation of thought to tone and tone to

thought as the chief aim, the writer bears witness to the fact that tone-building by means of exercises and a jargon of syllables was to him nothing but useless torture, and his settled conviction that the only way of securing effective voice is to trust to mind and reason. The student will therefore watch and listen whether his pronounced word reproduces the thought which is in the word, together with its atmosphere. When the sung word expresses an emotion without sentimentality, and displays colour without a trick—without distortion of larynx and mouth—the student is advancing. In place of the pitifully perplexed question which pupils often ask, 'Is that tone right?' if he think, breathe, and pronounce comprehensively he will, when the word falls upon his ear, find out if he is true to the thoughts entrusted to his care by poet and composer. All the 'right' there is—is in that truthfulness. Every fairly intelligent student ought to know when his tone is right if he use his brain.

In discussing this absorbing question of voice culture, thoughtful critics often express the opinion that singers, as a class, are not overburdened with brains. Singers have as much brains as other folk, but do not always use them. They depend on voice; pretty, pleasing, sensuous or loud voice. From the jugular tenor to the guttural bass is a far cry, and from both it is some distance to l'expression juste; yet a large percentage of singers have this journey to make; if they faint not they will at last find themselves in the neighbourhood of this same 'just expression.' It is true also that every ideal attained gives birth to another and a higher.

To the end that the student may secure that justness of tone as his chief aim, he will seek to rid himself of the rigid throat; will exercise himself both in speech and song; will travel and observe men and cities; will obtain personal experience of opera, oratorio, *Lieder* and the work of actors and orators. It is not unwise to mark down such artists as are simple and unaffected in their methods. Slowly obstacle after obstacle will disappear. The singing of poems by Goethe, Schiller, Heine and others, in addition to those of poets of the English school, will bring a justness of expression which cannot fail to affect the singer's tone. In course of time he will find that he can give spontaneous readings of any kind of vocal music. He who has been along it knows the road, and whither it leads; knows also that it is best to keep to the middle of it, not one day this and another day that, but ever in pursuit of a definite object. Holding these opinions, one cannot but regard with stern disapproval those who lead the blind astray. The teacher was not born to play the sphinx.

Having thus traversed the ground under the guidance of nature, it would seem reasonable to aim at some typical definitions, that the wisdom of the world of singing may employ itself on our conclusions, and, for the benefit of mankind, show us where we have gone astray.

## DEFINITIONS

### I

Singing is a natural, easy and controlled musical and poetic expression of an inner self which has been enriched by the creations of inspired men.

### II

To sing is to use all natural endowments for the expression of all natural thoughts, sentiments and emotions.

### III

(*a*) Singing is the result of the simultaneous activity of all physical, mental and spiritual elements through the medium of voice, for the purpose of musical expression.

(*b*) Singing is the unifying of the senses, the intellect, the soul and physical power.

(*c*) The act of singing is an energy of the human frame acted upon by the senses, mind and soul, for which voice acts as the medium of expression.

### IV

Singing is the outward, audible sign of inward spiritual mind.

### V

(*a*) A singing voice is the result of a compelling desire to sing.

(*b*) To sing is to reveal the varied objects of poets' and musicians' artistic regard and treatment.

(*c*) Singing is the vocal result of musical heredity, that is, of aesthetic and spiritual sensibility and of environment.

# VII

## STYLE

'THE STYLE IS the man,' for as the man is, so must the manner of his expression be. As there are men and men, there are styles and styles, and as there are stages in character-growth, so there are mature and immature styles. Every one who has familiarized himself with the ground-ideas of makers of history has introduced into his mind universal thoughts, which sooner or later affect his character. The thoughts of others also find a place in a man's mind, and an amalgam is made.

In music, as in the other arts, we speak of the classic and the romantic. There is in music also another style, neither classic nor romantic; an angry man might call it frankly brutal, sincerely vulgar, colossally ignorant. The modish company which affects this style would gladly annihilate all but those who take a metronome to represent rhythm. Most sure it is that the metronome has its uses, and most certain too that it is mechanical when serious work is to be done. Elastic and truly rhythmic *tempi* or beats, commodious and non-tyrannical, are better than spasmodic, juggernautish nods. An educated man's idea of time will show that he has been led out of mechanical ideas.

Before a man can acquire style he must read great books

and move among men and women who are accustomed to think. Symphonies and oratorios were not written for the special glorification of the unhappy and distressing personalities which find degeneration in the worship of themselves. An inelastic time-measurer cannot give us characteristic Bach or Beethoven, Mozart or Wagner. Metronome marks are never more than approximate at best. Rhythmic time, as all men know, is essential to style, and all good artists love their 'four in the bar.' But rejection of inelastic *tempi* must not run riot and develop into universal *tempo rubato*. It is certain, however, that genial and gentle men are far more likely to understand the musical writings of genial and gentle men than is the man who permits himself to become the *tyrant* of the conductor's stool. Pigmies cannot appraise giants, and pigmies cannot grow unless they be modest when listening to eminence as it speaks. Every personality of whatever sort must be enriched by lessons culled from great performances, and the greatest and noblest style is ever the simplest. The present writer can never forget Weingartner's exclamation behind the scenes at the opera-house in Berlin after a soul-stirring performance of Beethoven's *Pastoral* and Mozart's *Jupiter* symphonies. 'Children, we must seek to be simpler—ever simpler.' The study and discussion of style, however, have not infrequently been turned into mysteries and riddles. This helps no student, produces no artist, however remunerative it may be. A mysterious compound, this other 'style'; costly, and full of hocus-pocus. Let us endeavour to analyse.

The first ingredient we find in style is dominion over passion and frenzy. The discipline of emotions must be strict, and it must be our own discipline. If we desire to preserve originality our style must not be copied or taught.

True, we may be taught how to *teach ourself* style, but that is all the teaching that will be of service to us in the matter of how to do our work. Crescendo, accent, etc., must be the composer's, or our own. In the latter case mature thought is imperative; text and music must fit us, and we must do the fitting. Sartorial centres turn out good ready-made garments; they can never be anything but ready-made (one can tell them anywhere). 'In a multitude of counsellors there is safety,' say some; and one gives 'voice-production,' another 'diction,' another 'readings,' another 'style.' Not infrequently, however, the original thing which constitutes voice, diction, style and reading loses itself, and ceases to grow, while undergoing the different processes, and eventual possible eminence is supplanted by self-assertive mediocrity. Good masters are good gifts; but students try to substitute the master's labour for their own personal individual struggle. The brave and independent student allows his style to grow with him; deep thought and healthy self-criticism will bring a satisfying style. A sprinkling of accents and expression marks, pepper-box way, paralyses a man's effort and turns out stylish singers of low degree. 'A thin veneer of polish on a solid block of ignorance,' as a caustic Welsh cleric once said to some candidates for ordination.

A singer should read books on literary and artistic subjects; these supply him with illustrations. As he studies poetry and literature, any observant singer, especially if he read aloud, will observe how the mind works in its efforts to create a desired impression. In the work of a master of literary style there is no sense of hurry or of anxious grip, though there may be one of movement and of tense grasp. Word succeeds word with stately dignity, the crescendo is gradual and sustained, until the climax arrives. Poet and prophet create the picture which they see in their mind, and that mind having in the main a moral purpose sees the thing as it should be, and as it *is*. Denunciation is measured—prophetic. In the words of Samuel to Saul after the slaughter of the Amalekites the temper is dignified, for all its wrath. Samuel spoke for his office, which to him was sacred and not to be tampered with even by the king. It is an affair of kings and prophets, not of demagogues and priestlings. The case is the same when exaltation, and not anger, is the incitement to emotion. Whatever the emotion, the speaker, writer and singer must govern it justly and appropriately. This he will do if he give due attention to the predisposing causes of the action and of his comment thereon, as well as to the consequences which may follow both the action and his comment.

To study such matters is to produce to some extent a mental state similar to that of the poet as he wrote. Slowly the power of sifting grows, *especially as the student reads aloud*. Gradually the brain will assimilate the essentials of a fine delivery; for the poetic and the literary gifts are essentially musical. The student will not allow the mind to be led away from the subject at any point. If the temper be right, he will not be thinking too much of the action, nor of the comment or the state or the mood he is describing, or its effect upon himself or his audience. The good artist never thinks of himself or the effect he is producing, for he is not consciously trying to produce any 'effect.' Though fine effect is ever the result of fine art, like health it should be natural to one. To cure undue passion and exaltation, we should study the style of inspired writings. The theatre is a good teacher too.

Though passionate it must be, for without passion there is no art, general culture and observation help the student to discipline utterance.

Style must be straightforward and spontaneous. A stilted, halting, mincing, anxious, studied manner can never produce the powerful effect which comes with breadth and ideal realism. If art fulfil its mission, it will translate the artist into the realm of the real ideal, whose sights and sounds he will reproduce as straightforwardly and spontaneously as though he saw them with the bodily eye. His utterance will be easy and flowing, never far-fetched—by which one means that class of expression which is improbable and can only appeal to a crazy clique. One who has no spontaneity stops to consider what style will please the largest public, and will finally please no one worth the pleasing, will appeal to no one worth appealing to. The trick 'artist,' who cultivates a spurious versatility, has no real power at his back and sooner or later will be found out; one cannot 'deceive all of the people all the time.' Similarly, one may say, call no man a great singer until you see how he lasts, and in what capacity. While an unconventional art-product may cause bewilderment at first, and time for consideration and absorption be required for it, finally the true artist charges home, and remains there. Whatever message an artist feels it is his to give, let him give it directly and simply. He will have the right of holding his message true when he has thought long and suffered hard for it.

It is cowardly to abandon loyal and spontaneous utterance because, forsooth, it is hard to persuade some hearers that there may be superlative beauty in a new and unconventional conception. Once convinced that a certain poem, set to certain music, satisfies your highest artistic aspirations, never yield until your vision has been realized by the people. If you persevere you will reap the reward; if you make no effort you will become a mere wraith. We have heard it said, 'You must give the people what they want.' How often do those who conform to it have to change their bill and their cast! As well feed children upon sweets! *By all means give the people what they 'want,' but define the word yourself.* A singer who gives not what he desires to give but what the public clamour for is certain to fall a victim to a forced style. He will always be *trying* to say something. Nothing was ever said by trying in this sense.

The present writer once overheard the American robin practising his tune on successive days until he secured the intervals he desired, when it was easy to take down his tune. Here it is:

This bird was a great teacher in that he was a great and unconscious artist, and his song harmonized with life. He was apparently evolving a new tune or a variation on an old one. At first the notes came haltingly, but, after a long rehearsal, as surely as if they had been played on a keyed instrument. While he was unconscious of externals he sang; he knew what he wanted to sing, nor did he consider the songs of other birds; he clung to his own. A mere human being seated beneath incautiously imitated his song. Aware that he had an audience, the bird straightway ceased. He was singing to the sun, and not to any audience. No man, of course, could guess the instinct impulse in the bird's breast; and the imitation frightened him. It is the way with imitations; they *are* frightful. They destroy frank, spontaneous, simple melody which arises from a similar instinct, aided by imaginative reason, in man. Must all song then be entirely intuitive, and does tuition destroy style and frankness of expression? No; teachers are indispensable, and we can boast of many earnest men and women who devote their lives to the cause. Great indeed is the gratitude we owe to faithful masters—and greater loyalty!

To the discipline of passion and free expression given to original song as elements of 'style' must be added the faculty for compelling an atmosphere charged with spirituality. This does not mean the superficial affectation which has brought pretence and pretentiousness even into the churches—whence, one fears, it makes periodical pilgrimages to greet its relative on the stage. Ideal spirituality, or spirituality of idea, need not convey the impression that the performer feels himself to be a monopolist in divine and spiritual things—as though one said, 'I have penetrated the inmost sanctuary and bear a special mandate.' The spiritual idealist will be modest but earnest, having a quietly convinced and convincing air. A simple courage and a deep conviction will be about him and his voice. Caught up in the grasp of the imaginative reason, the student will in spirit cultivate the acquaintance of all characters sung by poets and musicians. These and their kind will nourish him with the far-reaching influence of their words and deeds. Living, moving beside and breathing the same air with men who have not yielded to the soft slavery of the present, students of song become similarly inspired. These are they who toil and fight that the future may become the present in prophetic realization of ideals.

The question of the adjustment of poetic and musical values, the matter of emphasis, accent, rise and fall, contrast and the like, must not be lost sight of. The giants of musical composition use prescribed accents, emphasis and expression marks sparingly. In miniature work one expects miniature directions; yet if the music is the text in another language, the accent must be somewhat akin in both; the emphatic word and note will be of equal power and value, except when the composer seeks to secure a greater effect by hastening or deferring the natural accent. Thoughtful study of text and music cannot fail to make it clear that the two are one, and that the resultant of the combined pair is just as much one thing as either taken singly. The expression of that thing will depend on mental discipline, and not on how many crescendo marks the composer is forced to add. On the other hand, the cunning master will set before his students models of a perfect union between words and music. In dainty and subtle lyrics every bar must be learnt and sung *exactly* as the composer has marked it, and this exact miniature work is of great value in establishing delicacy of touch. In such songs as Robert Franz has written every mark means something; the composer has with infinite patience and precise knowledge of poetic values worked with a magnifying glass upon every one of his songs. The student who sits down before them stores his memory with lessons of nice and spiritual expression, for they abound in such models of patient, sensitive, musical eloquence.

Our German neighbours never weary of insisting upon the necessity for 'pregnant consonants.' We may borrow the word and speak of a pregnant style. No style is mature unless it suggests more than it says. Once the finite fails to hint at the infinite, the singer holds no further interest for progressive humanity. When a singer can suggest more than he says, we may feel confident that he will not readily come to the end of his resources. Elasticity is one of the marks of creative, as receptivity of budding genius, where there are impressions to be noted and received. When students preserve the melody in each word and note, sentence and phrase, they cannot stray far from home. Especially, let them be independent of praise and dispraise. Style is a manifestation of character; the loftier the latter the more exalted the former will be.

For the singer a complete acquaintance with musical form is also necessary; the science of sound manifest in musical compositions must form the subject of separate study. Every singer should play some instrument sufficiently to enable him to acquire an exact sense of rhythm and pitch. The compositions of the great masters in some shape or other should form his daily food. The characteristics of the musical form of each master should in turn occupy the mind. The profound scholarliness of Bach, passionately religious, instinct with weighty and loud-resounding eloquence; the titanic might of defiant Beethoven, valiant apostle of humanity; the pomp and majesty of Handel; the geniality of Haydn; the lone genius of the gentle Mozart; the unfettered naturalness of self-tutored Schubert, the child of nature; the eclectic yet fervent self-absorption of the recluse Schumann, whose note is as much the note of a musical cloister as that of the busy haunts of men; the studious, lyric melody of Franz; the lofty, muttered themes of Brahms; the imaginative, literary, and significant strains of Wagner: all these attributes appertain to musical style and can be grasped only by a study of the works in which they appear. There must be knowledge of music *as music*, and skill of some sort as instrumentalists, or the singer's work will lack something which cannot well be put into definite words, but which we may roughly designate—musical atmosphere.

# VIII

## ORATORIO AND OPERA

ORATORIO AND OPERA performances are frequented by two separate classes of person who, in general, do not interchange their modes of relaxation. Owing largely to the influence of the prophet of Bayreuth, the echoes of operatic propagandism have filled the world. In Wagner's works, especially the later ones, we see that he was at variance with his predecessors except in so far as they had been loyal to ultimate truth of expression, that is, to such convincing expression as springs rationally out of the text and beyond which one could not expect them to go at the time. It was expression of this kind which stood for their share of the world's spontaneous utterance; nothing else had value in his eyes, and his imaginative reason refused all other modes of musical eloquence. Unless the succession of musical sounds constituting the phrase expressed musically and dramatically the same thing as the poetry expressed in literary form, he would have none of it.

Operatic verisimilitude would seem to depend upon some such theory as this, though the effect upon music of an unduly rigid adherence to this doctrine is perhaps hard to determine. Perhaps many music-lovers do not thoroughly understand Wagner, any more than they have as yet plumbed the depth of Bach. It is even possible that the great dramatic composer has not, in spite of his voluminous writings, explained himself, and that the full significance may dawn only when future generations have brought their light to bear upon his compositions. With the advent of a calmer view of his works, which time, improved conditions and technique alone can bring, the exact amount of profit and loss to the world's music arising from the reforms of Gluck and Wagner will be duly estimated.

The personal triumph of the personal Wagner is complete, and also, a thing which would have distressed him had he foreseen it, the triumph of the 'operatic' idea over the general public. Few indeed realize the difference between opera and music-drama, and not many are aware that Wagner abjured opera after *Lohengrin*. The general public listens to opera from the standpoint of pre-Wagner writers of opera, and not that of intelligent observers of the drama; and this public is liberally catered for. All the world wants to write opera, and accordingly —to quote the epithet of a distinguished Oxford linguist— the 'lunatic side of the operatic stage' continues. Although much that obtains on the operatic stage seems to spell lunacy in the opinion of scholars (and this should not be the case if opera were a finally typical form of art), yet to the large majority of the public it is a very pleasant form of lunacy; it amuses and entertains them. Had the world laid to heart Wagner's distinction between opera and drama, it would have cured itself long ago of the confusion between the two.

But which, after all, is the higher form of art and has produced the nobler music on the whole? Do social leaders ever ask this question? The event in every great metropolis is—a new opera! It is unfortunate that the value to music of this form of art should be so exaggerated. Other forms of musical development suffer, and a tendency toward making abstract music more and more articulate and concrete shows itself among composers.

The public must finally learn that, hitherto, opera has not made for the highest in music, either in regard to composer or performer. Many people will fiercely resent this statement. But it is not so terrible as it looks. Let us calmly consider the matter. It is not here implied that an operatic composer cannot attain to the highest music in his operas; our claim is that, as a general thing, he has not done so. Mozart's *Don Giovanni*, Beethoven's *Fidelio*, and Wagner's *Die Meistersinger* do not cover the whole of the ground, although the achievement in these three masterpieces stands supreme in the history of the lyric stage, and may be said to contain the promise of further achievement, which in the course of time will surely become more general. For nature is at work, and doubtless there will ensue a more adjusted, a truer balance between the aesthetic and spiritual qualities. When composers as such shall have secured greater freedom of action; when knowledge of effect and of the means of securing it enables the musician to put forth his powers under supreme control, though we perchance may not, our successors will possess more ideal operas and music-dramas than even those the world has hitherto put to its credit. After all, the world can afford the time for the task of producing a man in whom human passions and emotions shall have assumed a character farther and farther removed from the elementary one they possess in the animal man.

The brain of man, the upward journey once begun, has been separating him more and more from the lust of sheer

sensuous emotionalism. Through artistic evolution, using
the words in their highest sense, there must finally appear
sublimer types of spiritual passion, more and more remote
from, and less and less dominated by, animalism and
frenzy. Nature has already made brain superior to muscle;
small wonder if her next task be the production of such
a passion as shall have more of psychic than of physical
propensities in it. The musician of all people will benefit
by this advance, and so will operatic writers and singers.
But it will still be true that the loftier the theme the purer
the music. Oratorio will continue to hold its own,
musically, and in the end will reward opera for its efforts
in the direction of verisimilitude by absorbing and making
it one with itself. We must cease to separate activities
which will finally be seen to make for the same end. To
draw sharp lines between classicism and romanticism is
to weaken both. What the new form of art will be, no
man can tell; but we will presume to suggest to future
generations that a good title for it would be SYMBOL, for
we talk of the infinite in terms of the finite, and this is all
we can do.

Now opera-bred music-lovers are in general apt to be
fervent, scenic, dramatic—aggressively all three—in their
ideas of music. The operatic type is characterized by a
certain narrowness of vision, and we are all expected to
look through his spectacles. Dramatic verisimilitude is
indeed fascinating and absorbing. Instantaneous photographic illustration of poetry and drama with, and by
means of, music produces an effect so immediate and
moving that the ear, trained to listen for a quick corre-
spondence between poetic-dramatic thought and the music
which expresses it, becomes impatient of anything which
keeps action waiting, so to speak. The reproduction of

poetic-dramatic thought in musical form—the story, action, movement and histrionic 'character'—all those things demand some such treatment as Wagner gave to them in his works on lines which differed fundamentally from the methods of other composers. The music must not indulge in independent flights; it must ever wait upon the play when the *dramatis personae* are in evidence. Yet, though it be conceded that vain repetitions and gratuitous *roulades* and *fiorituri* cannot help to develop dramatic action as such, still the belief is justified that there exists a form of music which is far higher and purer than operatic music—in which the above-named considerations have been held paramount.

Degenerate and torpid *coloratura* music is doubtless of no value, and (to make a sudden excursion into oratorio) even the *coloratura* music of Handel, for example, fails in its purpose when sung as a mere vocal exercise. But it is practically certain that this particular form of musical expression was never intended for general use in the musical depicting of quickly moving, graphic and continuous drama. Nevertheless, it had and has its uses, as is proved by the fact that, in spite of the dull puritanical treatment to which it has at times been subjected, *Messiah* holds its own to-day, not only in the estimation of the public but of the most eminent musicians of the world. No one has hitherto disputed with Handel the honour of setting, in epic musical form, the Christ life as it is unfolded in scripture—though we read that the librettist thought the composer might have done better! And this music lives its own life, free and unfettered; it arose out of the situation just as truly as Wagner's music, and is moreover adapted to its high theme; is simple indeed, but capable of endless expansiveness.

It was, of course, vain to imagine that *coloratura* could be suitable to all kinds of sentiments and situations, especially those of a purely mundane character. The roulade lends itself with particular suitability to religious and purely heroic subjects, and to any situation indicative of a fixed mood, as, for instance, it was used by Ambroise Thomas in the Ophelia music of *Hamlet*. But while we may reasonably rejoice in the continuous development of drama, and revel in the pulsations of music which sways with every emotion of the heart and varies with every change of mood, we may also reasonably enjoy our contemplative, spiritual, religio-heroic measures, which owe their impressiveness as much to their inherent musical strength as to the subject-matter which they musically illustrate. In these measures are included *cantilene* and *coloratura*, whether of the vocal solo or of the multivoiced chorus. Wagner himself employs music of the oratorio type in *Parsifal*, and he never left out of his calculation the works of Bach and of Beethoven. It might indeed be suggested that opera and music-drama are good stepping-stones—are 'studies' for oratorio; at all events it was so in Handel's case, seeing that he composed operas for twenty years before launching out upon his wondrous work in oratorio.

Those therefore who gravely assert the superiority of operatic over oratorio music, *as music*, are victims of a mistaken notion, namely, that music is nothing if not histrionically scenic and excitingly illustrative (photographic would perhaps in some cases be the better word) when wedded to words. If the supreme test of music were its scenic and illustrative character, without any other characteristic, then indeed oratorio might be in bad case. But it is at least open to serious question whether this principle cannot be carried too far, so that some of the repose always inherent in music of an absolute, as well as a relative, character becomes lost.

Now all men know that vocal music comes into being when there is sustained verbal effect. The moment sustained periodic effect is desired (*to sustain with periodicity is to make music*), what artistic reason is there to forbid the sustained effect being prolonged, even though the composer use but one word for the purpose? To many a nervous, metropolitan, kaleidoscopic mind, which is constantly being turned upside down and back again, such a question would perhaps seem preposterous. An opera-enthusiast will say that 'it retards dramatic movement'—a cry which at one time, not long ago, cropped up with parrot-like frequency, and has not yet ceased. But music is music, even when there is no rapid unfolding of the tale; a fact proved by great musicians when composing to a few words, or to *one* word. There is, after all, such a thing as *musical* 'dramatic movement.' Modern restlessness discounts the value of prolonged musical effect, the mood of which need not be restless and ever-changing to suit the spirit of the age; nor is the music which has a word or syllable attached to every note necessarily superior to that which has not.

The music of 'Amore Traditore' and of 'Ich will den Kreuzstab gerne tragen' (to name one of the secular and one of the sacred cantatas of Bach) is surely worthy of the respect in which all good musicians hold it. The sustained *coloratura* and contrapuntal passages, and the reiteration of single words, all of which make up the whole of these compositions, cannot be dismissed as an artistic mistake. Deny the legitimacy of prolonged musical effect in conjunction with one word or one idea, and you deny the power of every fine solo, cadenza and chorus ever written. Because the contrapuntists of long ago, from whose vagaries Palestrina rescued Church music, went mad over their tricks, is that a sufficient reason why people in our day should refuse to acknowledge the reasonableness of contrapuntal oratorio?

All music is written for the sake of making an effect—to express an idea. Fugue, roulade, counterpoint, polyphony, harmony are all means which, when used rationally and artistically, produce a legitimate 'effect' and express some worthy musical thought. Let any composer try to write an aria on a short text such as 'Every valley shall be exalted and every mountain and hill made low'; without the aid of *coloratura* he would not get very far. Through Handel's setting of 'Every valley' we feel more fully the vital significance of the text than would have been the case without verbal repetition. Each repetition offers a new aspect, so that the inner meaning becomes gradually unfolded.

The simple truth is that roulade, cadenza, fugue are just as legitimate for purposes of musical expression and musical structure as the classic literary phrase 'kumatone anerithmon gelasma' (*ridentibus undis*—'the countless laughter of ocean'), used by Aeschylus in *Prometheus*, is legitimate for poetic expression. Both are derivative ideas, arising out of an artistic sensing of the situation; there is just as much 'reason' in the one as in the other, though there is neither 'reason' nor 'logic' in a roulade, *per se*, and it can of course be turned into a pyrotechnic display; not a very great deal to argue about.

It is not too much to claim that oratorio partakes more of the character of abstract music than does opera, and indeed than any music with which a dramatic text is associated. If the history of composition prove anything, it is that the *music which depicts a lofty mood is eternally superior to that which illustrates restless movement and action*. The higher the mood the higher the music—other things being equal. But to speak generally, while the oratorio enthusiast will always be in danger of the ponderosity of archaic formalists, the opera enthusiast is liable to be the prey of artistic sensuousness. With one form to correct the other, good taste and temper in art will finally ensue. Man is more the master of the situation, and of his powers, when he contemplates a mood than when he is hurried on by the force of an objective passion, which he not infrequently converts into a subjective one. On the other hand, the excessive tendency toward so-called realism seems in our day to degrade the language of music to the level of passing needs, and to rob it of that inscrutability which is ever the mark of high art.

To return, the perennial founts of musical inspiration have been Bach and Beethoven, whose leanings were toward oratorio rather than opera. Apart from their abstract music, they occupied themselves with sacred and kindred subjects mostly, and their works supply musicians with a standard to this day. The enlightened listener asks that modern music shall, in its degree, make the same *kind* of effect as theirs did and does; the laggard demands that the detailed *form* of their compositions shall be imitated. The classic purity of their work is due to the fact that they were content to give a simply musical expression to their musical ideas and instincts, and when they elected to associate definite extraneous thought with music, it was always 'thought' borrowed from the world of religion or heroic manifestations of the higher humanities. On the other hand, opera has hitherto been concerned mostly with

primitive excursions, *qua* drama, into the realm of sometimes elevating, ofttimes degrading, passion which supplies human life with some of its most alluring situations.
When first-rate composers deal with lofty subjects they
produce great masterpieces—pure, classic, simple and
spiritual in outlook. We should, therefore, hear the great
masters often, for a regular hearing cultivates a taste akin
to that of these masters.

Some writers declare, however, that classicism is
opposed to individualism in art. Naturally the individual
must grow or the race must die; individual growth matters
much, while racial through individual growth matters
more; and original inspiration (the emotional impulse-
maker of external origin) still more. Yet why do all sane
men love the works of the classic masters? Is it not because
they find them to be akin to themselves, as men; and in
the case of composers, because they find in them kindred
expression on kindred subjects. One need propose no
'tests'; these things claim us for their own, and we are
never more true to ourselves and to individual growth than
when we fortify ourselves with the spirit of men of classic
mould.

The mischief which produces copies instead of original
paintings creeps in when men repeat the accents or the
accidents of genius. There can never be any harm done if
musicians, by nurturing their powers of imagination, seek
to penetrate to some of the thoughts which forced the
giants to speak. These thoughts no man can learn except
through the classic masters' works. There will be, to be
sure, some pulling up of weeds by the roots, that space
may be found for the spread of universal thoughts of universal minds. Robert Franz spent the greater part of his
life in editing Handel and others. We are not aware that

his occupation interfered with his 'individual' growth. He did not sit down to write another *Messiah*, nor to evolve a new *roulade*; he simply produced his miniature vocal pictures, which albeit have that *something* about them which we are justified in calling the classic spirit. The fact is that the essence of classicism is love for an idea (the outcome of faith in a symbolic object) and the preservation of true balance between the architectonic thought and the play of senses and emotions; and, therefore, so to direct the activities of the latter by means of the former that men may realize the full effect of both.

Great art cannot live without the power—in those responsible for it—of mental absorption and the spirit of awe and reverence. A review of oratorio subjects will explain the presence of this spirit which makes itself felt. Whatever a man's creed, he is grateful if entertainment make him forget himself and his material surroundings. How much greater is the boon when we are transported to scenes that transcend in impressive power those which deal with ephemeral subjects. The things that have been in the distant past, the things that are to be, the mighty past and the still mightier future with their inspiration for universal mind, these make harmonious echoes in the breast of man and suspend the discord which Beethoven was fain to interrupt in the Ninth Symphony with 'Nicht diese Töne!'

What are the subjects which have given us the sacred works we may include under the term 'oratorio'? We shall give a fairly comprehensive list in citing: *The Passion*, which Bach treated with fine charity, so that the ordinary man might join his more gifted brother in its performance; the Masses; *The Mount of Olives; Messiah; Samson; Judas Maccabaeus; Israel in Egypt;* Mozart's *Requiem; Elijah;* Brahms's

*Requiem; The Creation; The Redemption* (Gounod), etc., and the works of the modern English school. If we add that operatic drama deals with the mundane aspects of love, hate, fear, etc., manifested for the most part under transitory conditions, this fairly covers the ground, if we except the *Ring of the Nibelungen*, which lies midway between the human and the spiritual. The mythological atmosphere of the *Ring* demands singing of a very high order, aesthetically, intellectually and technically. Oratorio drama, on the other hand, is concerned with the dealings of God with man; it sets Revelation in a strong light; creates through the intervention of the composer a sense of contrast, thus enhancing the power of the Word of God, and appeals directly to the spiritual side of man. The subject-matter of oratorio being what it is, an artist will discuss it with due solemnity.

Perhaps one can best emphasize the distinction between the dramatic elements in oratorio and opera by pronouncing the former to be religious and prophetic, the latter mundane and histrionic in character. The latter deals with man's attempts and struggles to secure advantages for himself or for his cause; the former with the manner in which man realizes the immanence of God in human affairs. With some such distinction before him any singer of average brain power will treat appropriately the musical and textual side of oratorio and opera, and this will be the easier in that the music is stamped with the influence of the subject-matter the composer has musically treated. For unless the atmosphere on the textual, as well as on the musical, side be reproduced, a distinct sense of discord and insincerity is at once apparent.

Much difficulty has been felt by composers when they **would** have placed the Sacred Person in character upon

the scene, and we have accordingly seen a narrator introduced because the thought of impersonation was felt to be
inadmissible. Yet, seeing that music is the fullest language
of humanity, it holds within it a power of 'revelation' and
of 'higher criticism' which is unique and valuable; whence
it has been said that one composer has brought the gospel
down even to our day by the vividness of his inspiration.
This is surely the kind of 'higher criticism' which most
men long for. If we introduce the phrase, 'Eloi, Eloi,
lama, sabachthani,' uttered 'with a loud voice,' as in
Bach's *Passion* according to St. Matthew, and the English
version, 'My God, My God, why hast thou forsaken me?'
which we find in Gounod's *Redemption*, the reverent artist
must, when singing these words, feel a deep sense of
responsibility. The solemn character of the text has before
now made an almost overmastering effect upon a singer
when called upon to utter this tremendous invocation.
But the work was there to be done, the impression to be
made, and with courage the singer probably bore himself
as bravely as he could.

Given a personality emptied of self and attention
centred in the work, art must become beautiful and unconscious, and this very unconsciousness will help to
develop a singer's technical power. Indeed, technique is,
in one sense, the highest offering a man can lay upon the
altar of art. He who has removed sensuousness of utterance
from his artistic creed, and has pinned his faith to the
truth that the sentient mind must sing, will have gone
some distance on his journey in art. He will have fought
for the power to produce a voice, just, true, and unhampered and will convey the words in such wise that the
soul of his audience will commune with itself and be still.
When technique enables a man to make an audience think

instead of applaud, the man and his technique are of some use to the world.

It may be necessary to repeat that the means whereby the subtlest gradations of mental work are conveyed from one mind to another are technical. All the reverence and spiritual exaltation in the world without technique are powerless. The unchanging condition of securing artistic results is hard, persistent work. To the subject of technique the writer has attended in his chapters entitled 'What is Singing?' For the rest, oratorios dealing with scriptural subjects, such as *Samson*, *Judas Maccabeus*, and others, may safely be left to the discretion of the thoughtful artist. By the aid of the imagination (and the very youngest pupils are easily awakened to the fascinations of the imaginative powers) any normal brain can picture the circumstances under which the characters he portrays lived and spoke; and also those under which the author and composer produced their work. It is a wise thing to familiarize one's self with the circumstances which gave rise to the work and with the composer's principles and artistic character, in so far as they are known. A singer's mind becomes subtler with every mental excursion into history, sacred or profane. All claptrap and meretricious effects will disappear.

The artist, as narrator, in oratorio gives the text a simple musical reading, which is only possible to a voice built on 'truth of expression.' The Herald in *Lohengrin* speaks dispassionately, as the King's mouthpiece, but with dignity and conviction. So in oratorio the narrator in the *Redemption* must deliver the text with sonorous and simply schooled voice. He will observe the musical laws and never sacrifice the balance and swing of a phrase for the sake of an *ad captandum* effect. Oratorio arias 'sing themselves,' as the saying is. Let the student read aloud the text, not disjointedly but with sustained effect, having first silently thought it—coherently. He must avoid jerkiness and the clipping of the second of two quavers; he should read the words to the pitch and time-value of the notes; according as they rise and fall, so will the voice be raised or lowered in pitch; the character of the literary phrase will thus rest musically upon his ear, with the emphasis designed for it by the composer's brain. The notes really represent the composer's way of saying, in music, what the words convey or suggest to him. Rossini's *Stabat Mater* has often been called inapt and incongruous. Why? Surely one reason is because great vocal art has been wanting for its due performance. 'Cujus Animam' and 'Pro Peccatis' can be sung in such wise that Rossini's idea of the words—that of a man who knew the musical tongue pretty well—becomes apparent without any of the glaring incongruity upon which such frequent comment has been made.

When singing recitatives the artist is permitted to exercise great freedom and elasticity, except in the case of those recitatives which have horizontal movement and not the simple vertical cord for accompaniment; just as in Wagner drama the recitatives are to be given with reference to the precise beat no less than to the literary form of the text, as Dr. Hans Richter has eloquently explained. This freedom is frequently abused; the recitatives in *Elijah* are much stronger as Mendelssohn wrote them than as many singers sing them. In oratorio is to be found also a type of singing which may be said to be midway between that of narrator and impersonator. It is something equivalent to the *chorus* in Greek tragedy. A solo, for example, which demands impersonal treatment is, 'Woe unto them!' (*Elijah*), which immediately follows 'Is not his word like a fire?' There should be no attempt made to express personal feeling in this aria; and certainly maudlin sentimentality is entirely out of place in reference to it. The singer is ill advised who takes the audience into her confidence and makes feeble moan with great head-shakings over the fallen prophets of Baal. Far better is it to stand apart from the tragedy and to make the pronounce-ment from a classic, even from an angelic, height. Such a pronouncement would be simple but terrible—a fateful comment upon a fateful situation. The atmosphere would then be one of aloofness, dignity, and impressive power.

Oratorios should be sung honestly, not meretriciously, from the standpoint of the Scriptures. Every singer should do his own singing, and not let someone else use him and his voice. A man's own brain and heart, once he has absorbed text and music, are all that he will find necessary for the best work he can do.

# IX

## ORATORIO AND OPERA
## (concluded)

WE KNOW SOMETHING of the 'prentice idea, historically.
Of old a lad who aspired to the dignity of becoming a good
workman served his apprenticeship to a master-craftsman.
Not much of this now, and as for skilled workmanship it
exists mainly as a name; machinery has destroyed most of
it, though isolated examples we may find. There was a
spirit of excess in the Reformation: it reformed the
monasteries with their technical schools out of existence.
Carving, illumination, and the like are crafts we know
but little of, and the spirit of work nourished by exactness
and precision, the love of and absorption in an idea,
because it was the all of those simple monks, is not ours
to boast of to-day. In pre-Reformation days the workman
did not waste much time in watching the market; he
devoted himself rather to the work and its completion.

Robert Browning has immortalized that *Pictor Ignotus*
of whom he sings. This painter—early in the sixteenth
century—had known the 'prentice stage; there is a comfort in the poem and a lesson to be learned of the impersonal, the unselfish, the objective in art. The 'unknown
painter,' who transferred an endless series of 'Virgin,

Babe, and Saint' to the 'damp walls travertine,' puts some of us to the blush. It is permissible to hope there are some spirits like his lurking in secret places around us. Perhaps we are at last awakening to the need of indulging in a little calm contemplation. To think closely and to bring our thoughts to a focus, so that we are absolutely unconscious of all surroundings; to know and see mentally nothing but what we have decided to concentrate upon, that is the essence of all fine effort, in life and in art.

We should love our 'trade'; it ought to be everything to us. Our 'prentice years need not affright us. It is more than possible that the thoroughness which was inseparable from the idea of apprenticeship enters largely into the character of that which came to be called *bel-canto* singing. The spirit of the time was a thorough and an exact spirit; trade was sacred, its product sacred, each man left something of himself in his work—surely the sanest thing he could do if he wanted to take a delight in his occupation. There is but little of this kind of sanity around us now. At this moment we seem to have 'run short of it.' Periodically a generation is liable to become unbalanced, and ours would seem to be no exception to the rule; nor could one in reality expect anything else, for our fate condemns us to do most of our thinking—upon the deepest questions—within sound of the clatter of the world. But the world does not want to stop and think in peace; it prefers to think on the run. To betray thought in work is to provoke much buffeting; the public must be 'amused'; art must give way to entertainment, opera is to be sung, money made, victim on victim found for the dragon. 'The march of civilization'! Is there not some little savagery left in it yet?

Burke said that the civilization of Europe depended for a long while upon two great elements, religion and gentlemanliness. These two principles—not their outward form but their root ideas—would ensure general truthful activity in music. Make-believe, snobbism and outward seeming without inward spirit have brought gentlemanliness—while cant and intolerance have brought religion—into disrepute; but snobbism should not destroy our faith in gentlemanliness, nor cant our love of religion. The artist is a unit in the picture, but he is not the picture, frame and all, though this would sometimes seem to be the case. Loyalty to art and composer will help every student to spend time and trouble while qualifying himself for his rôles. No student after a year or two spent in discovering how little he knows is qualified to give expression to the products of men of genius, who have devoted themselves throughout long years to the task of revealing their creative power in compositions of stirring, significant and profound inspiration.

Opera has affected the singer's art very deeply. The prominence of the position, the attractiveness of the situation, the play *plus* music and dancing, the scenery and the footlights, have made opera more attractive than concert or oratorio. Their vocal work and environment affect most opera-singers detrimentally; the result is unconsciously transmitted over the footlights to the singing and the non-singing public. Until Wagner appeared the work of the operatic singer trafficked largely with the mere senses. The form was effective but logically unreasonable. The set form of *aria*, *duo*, *terzetto*, and chorus was such as aimed at effectiveness at all costs. Operas throughout an extended period lacked the homogeneity which Wagner secured by being his own librettist. Not literature in any sense of the word were the books in most of the pre-Wagner operas. The Bayreuth master, following out to their fullest limit the ideas of Peri, Monteverde and Gluck in regard to melodic verisimilitude, made his dramas classic and intellectual as well as emotional. He drew upon literature, painting, poetry and music, and welded the whole into a mighty product of his genius, thus giving to the world a unique creation.

This creation demands from singers mental as well as physical powers; the latter are not wanting, but alone cannot counteract the conditions of the modern stage. Before Wagner appeared the insincerity and unreality bred of their work had produced their inevitable results upon the operatic art. As time went on vocal degeneration increased and a serious lowering of ideals ensued. When singers could deliberately stalk down to the footlights and address ear-splitting high notes to the gallery, the standard had become desperately low; persons became personages, the spirit was perverted, and the 'artist' became the point of observation, not the art. The true ideal of *bel-canto* had disappeared, and when the Bayreuth master called upon the vocal profession to sing his works an opinion came to be entertained that Wagnerian singing meant inevitable vocal-destruction. Instead of acquiescing in Wagner's contention that an artist is but a unit in the scene, singers made a rebellious attempt to secure prominence for themselves at all costs. Small wonder that much shouting prevailed, for by this time the art of thorough workmanlike singing was all but lost.

Self-assertion is destructive to singer and song in Wagnerian, as to actor and play in regular, drama. Wagner is akin to, and devoted to, Bach and Beethoven; when singers realize what this means, a reaction must set in. It has begun, though there is room for regret at the unnatural bellowings which are still hailed as befitting the character-painting melodies of the Bayreuth master. They will, however, finally destroy themselves, and as the teachings of *bel-canto* are gradually grasped once more, as the superiority of co-ordinate mental expression over sheer physical emotionalism is slowly vindicated, we shall ultimately have Wagner-singers of the type of the historic delineators of Shakespeare. So long as men think of and cling to voice as their first care, just so long will they neglect brain. The pretensions of vocal schools (Bayreuth and others) must go to the wall; even Germany must add the art of singing to her other musical excellences, so that her reproach in this connection may finally disappear. But though the singer's work in opera and drama has not hitherto produced its proper results on vocal art, we may safely hold that betterment will come, and largely through the instrumentality of the man who has wrongly been considered fatal to vocalists as such. His lofty ideals will prove to be lodestones, and will continue to attract the attention of earnest students.

The very aloofness, the very classicism of Wagner has supplied his critics with grounds for misrepresentation. Morality and decency, some say, have been alike outraged by his *libretti*. And yet Wagner made no sagas. He cast about for subjects which were highly dramatic; he was an Olympian, although he was also a very real volcano of Romance. His romance was, however, elemental, and it rose out of the situation; it was never forced. His purpose was the drama, and he needed extraordinary situations such as he found in myths, legends, and sagas to enable him to make musical comment upon man's destiny and the growth of his character. He accepted what humanity had preserved for him from the beginning. Time was his friend and treasury.

All Wagner's characters are extraordinary, and they produce extraordinary effects, musical and poetic, literary and well-chosen, impersonal and suggestive of universality. We do not cry out against Sophocles because of *Oedipus Tyrannus*, nor against Shakespeare because of *Macbeth*, nor against Browning because of *Pippa Passes*. So, surely, singers who deal with the elemental and the fateful must learn something of man's history and mythology, or their voices will scarcely fit the rôles provided for them.

If the singer of opera be not impersonal in his work and do not approach it as an artist, the dangers of the situation to him and to his art are enormous. The chief of these is a distinct tendency toward dwarfing his character, and from that follows the other, namely, danger to the voice. Unless the organ be grown to maturity from the smallest beginnings (the musical whisper) there would seem to be no arresting of the vocal decay which plays havoc with singers. If, however, we deal with this disorder *mentally* we can subdue it. Plato declared speech to be the important factor in music, rhythm and melody playing subordinate parts. This statement proves that the true ancients gave to thought-in-language precedence over the mere stirring of senses and emotions when combining words and music in one performance. That Wagner held similar views—being meanwhile fully alive to the claim of both senses and emotions—is clear from his dramas. He once made striking reply to a friend who, on being shown *The Ring* when it was finished, exclaimed, 'But there is not a note of music here!' '*Oh*,' replied the dramatist, '*that is nothing—the music is in the words.*'

The mind can and must, through concentrated imagination, discipline singers' powers and bring them into a state of quick activity, so that their vocal technique will finally be found ample for the performance of song, oratorio and opera. Then, too, it will be seen that Plato and Wagner have not joined hands in vain in regard to the supreme importance of the text.

The great lesson for singers in the whole process—from the earliest instances of the combination of words and music to the latest example of music-drama—lies in the fact that the process has been an evolution and that it bears an educational significance. As in the case of physical types, the variant forms remain while the constant disappear; so in regard to the product of the mental side of man the types which represent the greatest accumulation of psychic differences, and promise best for humanity, have survived; the mental growth of the individual is the formful result. Music and singing are at bottom such mental or psychic functions, and nature has not been idle in regard to them.

In the earliest instances of the combination of words and music, the solo voice—at this time no doubt the *vox diastematica* (held in check) attributed to the ancients by Peri in his preface to *Eurydice*—was the important thing, though the twanging music of the lyre accompanied it. But when she had once conceived the idea of using words and music in combination, Nature proceeded to make use of the fruits of her labours. Counterpoint and harmony had been evolved out of diaphony and descant, thereby enriching the science of sound, which had already absorbed the accumulation of slight differences of tone due to international communications (musicians wandered a good deal in those days as they do in our own). But in the delightful task of combining words and music for performance, it was found that *one* voice, even when accompanied by an instrument, became tiresome, and to avoid monotony—a sound art principle—many voices were now introduced. Accordingly we find that those who discovered the germ of the operatic and musico-dramatic idea (combining poetry, music and dancing for episodical entertainment) made use of their knowledge of counterpoint and harmony by employing many voices in situations where a single voice had, at one period, sufficed. In course of time this contrapuntal activity was carried to excess and its victims were landed in a dry-as-dust pretence; and though counterpoint secured rich sounds and a lively sense of movement, it finally dawned on the minds of the Florentine reformers that there was something wrong in the substitution of many voices for one, when the object was to secure truly dramatic individual expression. Accordingly a return was made to first principles, and the solo voice came to its own again as the only true medium for conveying the idea of individual action and characterization upon the stage. It had been ousted from its legitimate position in order that musical developments might be fully used, and having discovered that these rich things which music had been hoarding could be made use of in the accompaniments, there began the departure which ultimately proved so effective in the works of Wagner. This was made possible too by the growth of the orchestra, which in the days of Monteverde reached the respectable total of thirty-nine instruments, strings, wood and brass complete.

The style of the single-voiced artistic utterance to which the Florentines through Peri gave birth was called the 'representative' style—a bid for *l'expression juste* in composition. It was eloquent and histrionic, and all dialogue was treated in this way; it was, moreover, accompanied. But the conversion of this *musica parlante* into regular *recitative* and *aria* was reserved for Cavalli, the favourite pupil of Monteverde. Now Peri had records to help him—those dealing with the two modes of vocal expression in use among the ancients, the *vox diastematica* (held in check) and the *vox continuata* (the speaking voice). This *vox continuata* was probably perpetuated in a nobler form after a lapse of one hundred and twenty years in the *Recitativo Secco* of Mozart. Singers had by this time learned how to combine the *vox diastematica* and the *vox continuata*, with the result that they gave us recitative as we know it—or did. Peri in turn by using both, and by careful consideration of the potentially musical character of ordinary Italian speech, helped to evolve the comparatively histrionic and fully sustained voices which, later on, gave glory to Italy. It was on the inflections of the *musica parlante* that he even based his harmonies. When later on Cavalli drew a sharp line between *recitative* and *aria*, the singer's art, as such, must have grown; and we read of singers of that day becoming so exuberant in their vocal capacity that they introduced embellishments to relieve the 'monotony' of the situation.

This was a perfectly natural instinct in the 'singing bird'—and justifiable were there no intellectual reason against it—to indulge in some such embroideries as the *giri e gruppi* (flourishes and turns) with which Signora Archilei graced, or disgraced, Peri's score. But though there be some lovely melodies in the earlier examples of opera, much that was arid and uninteresting also meets the ear. Melody of an exalted kind was scarce, and so the irrepressible *prima donna* took out a licence, as is sometimes done, to kill someone else's game. Singers 'took the town' even in those days, and became indispensable, and took, besides, liberties with the composer's intentions.

It is more than probable that many a fine roulade and cadenza was thus invented. The singing instinct is a wondrous thing, and some composers have profited by it. But it is certain that the habit of irresponsibly 'embellishing' composers' works went much too far. Singers aimed at pyrotechnics, created a demand for them, and people flocked to listen. Good for the box-office and bad for art! Gradually, however, a wealth of melody ensued that could be used formfully and intelligently. The honest labour and thought spent on counterpoint must have helped to develop the ripe melodies which in Purcell's and Handel's days reached such extraordinary splendour.

The student of the growth of opera and of voice has therefore seen the singer start his journey with the use of the single voice; lose his way to the land of true personal expression; and finally reach a place where he could begin to cultivate artistic utterance. He arrived here only when he began to realize whence he came, whither he was going, and what the object of his journey. Leaving behind him much that was useless and uninteresting, the voice ultimately became a far more glorified medium of communication than it had been. If we examine the *typical* works that survive and still claim the regard of musicians, we shall find most of the things that have helped the singer to progress. The compositions based on occasional utility and effectiveness helped him as vocal exercises, and then died. They were musically helpful also, for musical compositions always reap benefit from the invention of new forms and methods of expression, while voices have certainly been vastly helped, as to their management and range, by the development of the science of music through counterpoint, harmony, and polyphony. Moreover, the use of the voice in choral singing paved the way to dominion over the difficulties incident to solo singing—when at last the individual voice resumed its position, and when singers found they had to deal with sustained melody, instead of that which we may justly call a musical and colloquial utterance. There is a gradual ascent from Peri and Monteverde to Wagner. The works of these two composers, and of Gluck, Mozart, Beethoven, Wagner, remain *reproductive in character and variantly typical in form*; and now man, with whatever knowledge he possesses, gathered through universal history, decides that all that is worthy of preservation is the work in which the *outward effect is correlated to the inner and truthful workings of a comprehensive mind*.

IT IS NOT TOO MUCH TO SAY, IN VIEW OF THE WORKS OF THE COMPOSERS (OPERATIC AND DRAMATIC) ENUMERATED ABOVE, THAT THE HISTORY OF OPERA FROM PERI TO WAGNER IS THE HISTORY OF THE REBELLION OF TYPICAL OR CHARACTERISTIC THOUGHT AGAINST THE TYRANNY OF THE SENSES—NOT TO THE ELIMINATION OF THE DUE EXERCISE OF THE SENSES, BUT TO THE ENTHRONEMENT OF TYPICAL THOUGHT AND IMAGINATIVE REASON ABOVE THEM.

Personal vagaries were abundant in vocalists' performances until the growth of the orchestra in effectiveness; the luxuriant development of melody and the inclusion of turns, trills and roulades in the scores of men like Rossini made singers' interjections redundant and superfluous. Gluck, Mozart, Beethoven and Weber had written their strong dramatic works, and Bach and Handel had said their say in other directions, so that the constant and unobjective appeal to the senses showed signs of coming defeat. Embellishments which the voice had formerly arrogated to itself began to appear in the orchestra; counterpoint enriched the sonority of the music; the 'accompaniments' became richer. These developments continued until at last Wagner propounded once more the theory that opera, if it was to be true in expression, must be, first and foremost, emotionally and linguistically truthful—that is, must be based on rational and imaginative utterance. In addition, whatever legitimate appeal could be made to the senses by the introduction of the principle of horizontal harmony into the orchestral part of musical drama, Wagner made use of as a means of reaching the higher qualities in the hearer's intelligence; and the same may be said in regard to the voice part. The great musical dramatist cared little for the emotional appeal as such; with him it was a means to an end. His great idea was to set character in the making on the stage, to illustrate—nay, to 'represent,' in the representative style beloved of the Florentines and of the Greeks before them—a scene or a human or ultra-human being in the course and at successive moments of development, and to mark the path of fate.

Wagner-drama makes the senses subservient to objective thought; the actor-singer must keep his mental eye fixed upon the character he is representing. There must not be even a momentary lapse from this position. Each character is clear-cut and formful or typical; each utterance typical of that character, each action a manifestation of it. If singers therefore are to learn the lesson which Wagner taught the world, they must take their stand upon the principles which he advocated. These principles, with his original musical genius, enabled him to realize the spirit that animated the men who gave us Greek drama; the same principles, with his intuitive insight, helped him to differentiate between the *spirit* of the Greek dramatists and the *form* in which they and their successors had expressed themselves. For mankind is forgetful of its own past and its lessons.

Yet for the most part operatic singers are not of much value in the singing of Bach and of Handel. Why should they not be? If the acquired thought in the brain first dominate the personality, then their technique (evolved by the necessity of uttering that thought with appropriate atmosphere) will enable vocalists to sing opera to-day, oratorio to-morrow, and songs the day after—and to be equally effective in all three.

The result of adopting Wagner's method is the substitution of truth and correlation to thought in the voice for merely aural, sensuous 'beauty.' The really beautiful technique necessary to secure truth and correlative thoughtfulness will ensure all the 'beauty' that is wanted to open up the avenue of the senses, that the depth of the hearer's understanding may be reached.

# X

## CONCLUSION

●

IT WILL BE profitable to note how far the vocal art of our time conforms to the higher demands of music that have been here discussed. Some of the most obvious demerits of operatic and dramatic singing are:

1. The sacrifice of truth of expression to size of tone. When sound is poured in cataracts, rational appreciation has perished. Ears and minds become artistically demoralized; moreover, one artistic ugliness paves the way for another. There is a limit to the size of tone if it is to be meaningful, a speaking and true tone. Love of sensationalism and the survival of the aim which singers cherished in early days—to stand out at all costs—destroys the value of the text as a medium of intellectual intercommunication; if one were to try to think and to get a coherent grasp of the character as the composer has drawn it, the task would often be found an impossible one. Din and confusion are essential to farce; but they are fatal to a serious play. It will be said, perhaps, that the conditions are wrong; but this does not weaken the force of that which has been advanced.

Many a weary cry has been heard issuing from the operatic stage. That it entails untold distress to sensitive natures has been made painfully apparent before now.

Fierce feuds are by no means uncommon behind the scenes of an opera-house, where yet they play the parts of gods and goddesses! *Tantaene animis caelistibus irae!* In some few cases much gold, abundant applause, and appreciation follow. Not much solid satisfaction even in these when a man has to face his own company, alone!

Formful words and characteristic atmosphere are the essentials of drama. Even gods in human guise, when condescending to walk the stage, should give us human language and not inhuman jargon. In the large tones of nature the largeness is one of depth, truth, reasonableness and justness. No one need be hostile to large tones as such. A man may sing with a noble godlike voice and be an artist, but there will be no sensationalism. The moment vocal quality is vitiated, and linguistic purity, musical meaning and poetic interpretation are marred, that moment the *raison d'être* of the human voice is ignored. If any man want a standard whereby he may judge how large a tone may be, let him take the words of the text as his guide. If he cannot pronounce the words as he would pronounce them were he a cultivated actor, his tone is too big.

2. The cultivation of so-called 'vibrant' tone is another error into which singers (men especially) are apt to fall. Immature criticism often singles out this quality for praise. 'Vibrantness' is the extreme, the mean of which is due vibration. By vibrant too many people mean, in reality, *vibrato*. A vibrant voice in the true sense is, of course, desirable; but such a voice is a very different thing to the annoying, distracting, little-souled, superficial-natured pretence which often does duty for it. *Tone, as we have pointed out, is an indication of character.* We are in no doubt as to the principles which go to make a fine man; why

should there be any uncertainty as to the principles under-lying the production of tone characteristic of that man? We might do worse than call tone a ready and expansive medium of characteristic expression. The ear attuned to literary, poetic, spiritual expression will always be dis-tressed by that quality which is popularly called vibrant.

Take, for example, some of the situations which call for incisive, truly vibrant tone, rich and sonorous. In the last act of *Carmen*, José's voice, if it is to convey the murderous mad despair of the discarded lover, must be vibrant in the true sense. In too many instances it is a case of the situation dominating the singer, and not the singer the situation. A singer should be so schooled that he can preserve artistic and aesthetic balance, that the tone may be true and just in the wildest upheaval of passion. Would it not be the highest kind of praise if one could say after the performance, 'The pity of it, that so fine a nature as José's should be dragged in the mire!'

The tone which would give rise to such comment would be produced by the whole man, organically; the whole mind and body would be in it. The catastrophe must be made clear; but the catastrophe of a deep, strong soul is artistically, aesthetically and spiritually higher than that of a shallower nature. José is a man of some breeding and dignity, possessed of gentle qualities. The terror inspired by the anger of such a man, mentally and physically ex-pressed, organically manifested, would be a better thing of its kind than the simply brutal anger of a jealous man. Vibrant operatic tone is too often brutal, and uncon-vincing.

3. Again, too many singers of the *open-tone school* rejoice in an artificially 'frank,' 'spontaneous,' and 'easy' pro-duction. This manner of voice always has breaks and spots

in it, and has to be treated for these spots and breaks. It is eminently easy to teach this kind of voice-production. With a fresh voice, in a month or two you can make such changes and produce such ready results and effects that the uninitiated will applaud and cry 'Marvellous!' A certain kind of 'breadth,' a cheap big 'tone,' and the power to express in a certain 'open,' 'frank' and 'manly' way (neglecting the fundamentals of the vocalist's art) are the easiest things in the world to secure. But the easy way is *always* wrong.

The greatest vocal danger of the open-tone school is that familiarly called 'the wobble.' Any singer who has no deep control of breath, and who sings with a so-called fine, open easy method, can secure a beautiful wobble, which will show itself immediately he is 'touched'—just as a Chinese china-mandarin wags its head at the slightest contact. The open-tone school is also open to another objection; it always becomes blatant, ranting, and scolding in character when the *dramatis personae* has denunciatory pronouncements to make; and it necessitates the carrying about of two voices if any attempt be made to sing on the concert platform.

With such a voice 'The Wanderer' in *Siegfried* would turn out to be a tiresome bore of an angry godling; aggressive, a personal fumer, strutting, frightening to dwarfs and women. The subtle comedy of Wagner's creation, the suggestion of the fate which stalks at the side of the god, the coming triumph of fearless faith over material resources, and a shadowy Valhalla, would not be in evidence. The chief thing would be the production of such a blare as would triumph over a hundred instruments. Nemesis is close at the heels of all such as would out-trombone trombones and out-cartilage cartilage. The lion has the shape for roaring; it is for a man to sing. A singer's tone should agree with the thought, and ranting and bluster cannot be considered the notes of the gods.

4. This 'open-tone' school has its opposite in that of the *closed-tone*. Both open tones and closed tones are necessary, but neither kind can be accepted, especially when they are vocally inevitable, as a legitimate type of singing. The Germans call these two styles 'light' and 'dark' singing respectively. If a man adopt the light or open method (women singers lean mostly to it), he cannot vary his tone-colour to any extent. No matter how many rôles he may undertake, vocally pretending to be, say, Mephistopheles, Daland, Leporello, or King Henry, though the rôles differ, the voice will be the same, 'splendidly null'—or 'faultily faultless' if the organ be naturally a fine one. There will be no real *chiaroscuro*, and when any copious histrionic demand is made upon the singer his vocal technique lands him on the rocks. Many a good plain singer, who can wake the echoes with a manly voice, complains, 'I cannot sing softly; all the vibration goes out of my voice when I attempt it.' But the *closed-tone* is chiefly effective in preventing the singer from making any spontaneous utterance. When a singer 'takes the veil' (closes his tone), and attempts to sing a phrase which demands simple expression and the just tone or quality which a true actor or elocutionist would use, he finds that the veil interferes with both mental vision and power of utterance. One must, of course, be able to veil the tone, as one would use a stop on the organ; but the tone must be veiled because we choose to veil it, and not because it chooses to veil us.

5. Again, certain gifted types of singers are liable to

sacrifice everything to artificial and sensuous enjoyment. They who possess 'charm' and an 'engaging personality' frequently abandon the higher self to these dangerous possessions. By 'higher self' of an artist is meant the mind, as a whole, which is capable of dealing characteristically (in an objective sense) with varied subjects. Charm and personality are reacting forces, and avenge themselves on art, artists, and public.

The harper in Goethe's *Wilhelm Meister* speaks of *wrong* as a force 'avenging itself on the earth.' The qualities we are considering, simple enough in themselves, become tyrants when men bow down and worship them. And the earth suffers because of their despotism. They breed sensationalism (an old enemy to art) which avenges itself in many ways on the singer. It narrows his views and stunts his growth; limits his sphere and damages his voice. When a singer discovers there is a 'charming' spot (as there is in many a voice) in his vocal range, and that spot proves effective, he notes it and puts up a signpost with the legend, 'Here I can let myself go.' And there, for some few years, he pours forth something which he and his hearers call 'tone,' in great plenty. The method arouses applause; his friends cry, 'It was great.' Strange how this kind of art induces a sort of mental paralysis! A certain kind of emotionalism, so the scientists tell us, *is* paralysing. Nevertheless, the *tour-de-force* is often requisitioned. 'The management' is glad; the voice and the artist suffer. The voice becomes spotty; the balance which should characterize all voices from top to bottom is disturbed; the range is curtailed and really expressive singing becomes an impossibility; *cantabile* effects are no longer feasible. The wreck becomes apparent when the singer attempts anything outside the range of the usual run of 'effective' excerpts, for which an undiscriminating public craves and clamours.

Such mannerisms being found to be lucrative, it is easy to fall a victim to the 'tricks of the trade.' The fate of such a one is sad from the vantage ground of sincerity of aim. Finally the public tires of everything. Star casts fail to draw. There is nothing more to throw to the lions; everything has been sacrificed. The vengeance of charm, personality and vocal effectiveness is complete upon those who have burnt incense in their honour!

The first thing for the artist is to decide that the lot of the slave is unhappy. A singer to whom the world owes a good deal once said to the writer: 'Remember, the public is the servant; the artist is the master!' The public must learn that it is not the master. The people are to be served, it is true, from the point of view that they must be educated. A good artist is ready to spend his life in the service of mankind. He will entertain and amuse his fellows, but he will refuse to be changed into a sentimentalist or a clown. He is the servant of art, and in that service he will suffer and dare all things—even to defying the world for the sake of ideals. Having emptied himself of himself he may leave the matter to work its way. An ecclesiastic once said, 'When people praise you and your sermon, you may know you have failed. When they dwell on the truth you sought to convey, you may know you have succeeded.' A singer may paraphrase and say to himself: 'When people praise you and your singing, know that you have failed. When they discuss the composer's message and art, know that you have succeeded.'

An unselfish singer cannot fail; he *must* succeed.

FINIS

# INDEX